Bliss
(ters)

How I Walked from Mexico to Canada One Summer

Gail M. Francis

ISBN 978-0-9966057-0-0

Dedicated to Michael George Landsberg

April 22, 1970 – May 18, 1995

CONTENTS

ACKNOWLEDGEMENTS

I thought about avoiding writing acknowledgements alto-gether, because once you get started where do you stop? I am too indebted to too many people to be able to properly enumerate my gratitude. But some certainly deserve special attention for the effort they made to help bring this book to fruition: Ken Paff, Sarah Dye, Jim West, and Marc Fendel (Gourmet), for example, for their feedback on the early ver-sions of the manuscript. Ann Francis Jenson read multiple drafts and shared an early version with her book club. I can invariably trust her advice about anything I write, and any-thing else for that matter. Knut Skarsem provided most of the photos, gave feedback on the manuscript, and allowed himself to be written about in some detail. Arianne Peterson invested considerable time and energy walking me through the many design considerations, and then doing whatever was best to bring the book to life—*Bliss(ters)* would not have ever made it into your hands without her. And Shane al-ways sets the table, no matter what project I've taken on: this book is the least of the things that would be impossible without him.

THE BEGINNING OF A TRAIL

The sun's first rays blanched the Texas desert's palette as my friends and I hauled ourselves up a ridge in Big Bend National Park. The cool air of February's pre-dawn hours still lingered on the shaded side of the mountain, but the labor of ascent drew sweat to our skin.

I dislike waking early and said so. Another hiker complained that more caffeine should have preceded the venture, and a smoker in the group gaspingly pointed out that she was too out of shape for this sort of behavior. But when we crested, the panorama silenced us all. I took in the eerily beautiful badlands sprawling below, and then I caught sight of something that would change my life.

A little red tent perched atop the next ridge. No roads led that way. The owner had to have carried that tent up there in the backpack now propped against a boulder. As I watched, a man unzipped the tent door, stepped out, stretched, and made himself a cup of coffee. Then he strolled over to the edge of a cliff and watched the final rays of sunrise. I wanted to do that.

But I didn't do that. Like many urges and impulses that require a step into the unknown, I figured I'd get around to becoming a backpacker later. Except within a few months something else changed my life: my friend Michael Landsberg died.

The Fates had been gentle in their selection of my first love. Mike's generous, gentle, and adventurous spirit continues to enrich my character to this day, though lichen now grows on his tombstone. Shortly after returning home from a Peace Corps assignment in Togo (in West Africa), he pulled out in front of another car. The impact killed him instantly.

Mike had always been so much braver than me, always eager to try something new. I promised myself that I wouldn't let these qualities lie buried in a grave, but rather would push myself to incorporate them into my own manner of living. Not long after the funeral I called our mutual friend Kris to see if he would be interested in a backpacking trip. Throughout the late 1990s and early 2000s, Kris and I logged almost 1,000 miles on the Appalachian Trail in the eastern United States. I also took solo trips or joined other friends on backpacking trips all over North America.

I learned from other hikers about the Pacific Crest Trail, which runs along the spine of mountains between Mexico and Canada. It begins near San Diego, then traverses the lengths of California, Oregon, and Washington before winding up in British Columbia. At 2,670 miles, it is one of the great trails of the world.

I have always loved the sparse, rugged landscape of the American West. On the Pacific Crest Trail, a person can at times hike for days without crossing a road. The remote path moves from wind-swept desert to high alpine peaks, through ancient forests and over blue-ice glaciers. A hiker on the PCT treads the habitat of cougars, bears, and rattlesnakes while navigating exposed ridges with sheer drop-offs or fording rivers swollen with spring runoff. From the first moment I learned of this trail's existence, I was drawn to the beauty and the challenge.

In my late 20s I came close to taking the plunge and attempting the hike, but at the time I was married to a man who couldn't bear being uncomfortably warm, at least not for the length of time it would take to traverse the desert sections of Southern California. I considered going solo, but

I let myself be persuaded by his claims that he could no more bear my absence than he could the desert. Ironically, little more than one year later he was the one who abandoned our relationship under circumstances that left me without the financial or emotional resources for a trip of such magnitude.

Over the years I continued to backpack, but with less frequency. In my mid-30s I bought a piece of land in northern Wisconsin with my partner at the time, Jessica. Living right in the wooded beauty of the northland every single day reduced the urgency of my desire to tramp around with a backpack. In fact, I became so attached to my 40 acres of heaven that I struggled to tear myself away for any length of time.

Yet, the dream of the PCT still nagged at me. By the time I was 39, Jessica and I had split up and she now lived in Baltimore. I had accumulated some savings and, with no major responsibilities and no major impediments, the reasons to put off a hike dwindled. I am not one of those naturally athletic people. I knew if I didn't try the PCT soon, my window of opportunity might disappear.

Just before my 40th birthday, I quit my perfectly good job working as an analyst for environmental groups and decided to give it a try. I brought certain weaknesses to the endeavor: outdated gear, inexperience in both desert and high alpine navigation, about 15 pounds of extra body weight, and a history of problems with my feet and knees. I also brought a few strengths: the ability to be emotionally self-sufficient, a feeling of comfort and competence in the backcountry, and a tendency to stay calm when problems arise. I hoped these qualities would carry me far enough to at least make a good showing.

A few facts about the Pacific Crest Trail: It begins near the tiny desert town of Campo, amidst a swarm of Homeland Security personnel. It ends in a forested wilderness at the border between Washington state and British Columbia. Yester-year's far-sighted conservation pioneers and today's far-sighted conservationists are to thank for its existence.

When Congress passed the National Trails System Act in 1968, the PCT was one of the original trails envisioned, though it took decades to complete. The route so frequently gets flooded, burned, and re-routed for dozens of other reasons, it's hard to call it ever truly completed, but since 1993 there has been a discernible path and an official route for the entire 2,700-odd miles.

Roughly 800 people attempted to hike the entire trail the same year I did, though the number of annual thru-hike attempts is growing rapidly. Typically about 60 percent of hikers make it the entire way. According to the Pacific Crest Trail Association, at least 2,600 have succeeded in completing the hike. By comparison, somewhere around 3,000 people have climbed Mount Everest.

The overwhelming majority of hikers, myself included, start in the south and head northward. Only a few hardy folks are willing to rush southward in time to cross central California's High Sierras before winter storms hit, and to arrive in an extraordinarily dry Southern California at the end of summer.

I spent my late-winter free time putting together 13 food packages that would be mailed to me along the way. In some cases the packages would be sent to businesses near the trail that agree to hold them for hikers. In other cases they would be addressed to me care of General Delivery in a given town, in which case the post office would hold them.

On March 13, I chucked my backpacking gear into my 21-year-old Honda Civic (odometer already reading 219,000), said goodbye to my little farm in northern Wisconsin, cried as I hugged my dog and cat, then turned the place over to house-sitters for the next six months.

As the miles accumulated southward, March became a time-elapsed video of spring. Literally by the hour I could see the changes as first the snow disappeared, then a few bits of green grass emerged. Next some roadside trees displayed buds, then leaves, and eventually flowers sprang forth.

That night at Iowa's Nine Eagles State Park, my performance would not have inspired confidence in anyone placing money on my eventual success on the PCT. As night settled in, dogs barked in the medium distance.

I am not afraid of bears. I am not afraid of cougars. I am not afraid of psycho killers. I am afraid of wild dogs.

When I was a child, wild dogs attacked our house. Americans of a certain age might recall a terrifying episode of Little House on the Prairie in which the Ingalls family suffered a similar misfortune. I don't doubt the two narratives have merged in my mind over time. I can't say how accurate my memory is, but what I recall is my mom slamming the inside door of the kitchen just as a German shepherd tore through the screen door. I recall sinister canine eyes sizing up the windows while pacing the side porch. More than my own fear, I recall the fear of my older siblings and the seriousness with which my parents assessed the situation. The end of the story involved my father and a .22 rifle.

The campground held only my lone tent that night. At 10 p.m. a truck passed along the drive and out to the main road. I heard the engine idle there a moment, then the clang of a gate being locked shut. The dogs renewed their savage calls.

I didn't want a sleepless night, so I attempted to take my mind off fear by counting sheep, but each time one jumped over my imaginary fence, canines ripped it apart. I reminded myself that instances of campers being savagely attacked by feral dogs in the middle of the night are so rare as to not even be a searchable statistic. Eventually I managed to fall into a fitful slumber, from which I abruptly woke when a bark rang out from the ravine below. Way too close! I fled the tent and dove into the car. When the sun shone through the windshield the next morning, I shamefully packed my belongings.

Gail 0, Fear 1.

From Nine Eagles I continued south, not immediately toward the Pacific Crest Trail, but to Arkansas for a seven-day training hike on the Ozark Highland Trail.

This splendid trail more than held my interest with its many gorgeous overlooks, historical areas, and stunning waterfalls. On the fifth morning, my water filter malfunctioned and I didn't want to risk contaminating the cartridge by trying to repair it with my dirty hands. I still had enough water to get to the next major water source, where I figured I would use one of my backup water purification tablets. When I got to that stream, I took the ill-advised step of reading the instructions on the package. I had previously failed to notice that these tablets required a four-hour time period for purification rather than the 30 minutes to which I was accustomed. I assumed that in four hours, I would already have reached a spot ahead that had potable water from a tap and so I just passed on the water altogether. However, with the leaves off the trees and miles of strenuous uphill on an intensely sunny and humid 85-degree day, I began to realize that without water I was a candidate for heat-stroke. Remember I am from northern Wisconsin, where we can go years without seeing much of that type of muggy weather.

Fortunately, I ran into a young couple who gave me some of their water to get me the final way. This is the only time I've taken water off another hiker. It's pretty low to be so unprepared that you have to mooch off someone who is likely also trying to conserve fluids. In this case, however, my benefactors were dragging a cooler as well as carrying packs, so I expect their needs were more than met.

Within a few miles I arrived at a campground. Lo and behold, the people who had given me water showed up in their SUV. They had decided to abandon their backpacking plans for the night. Since they were new to the activity, they had a number of questions for me and we chatted. At this point I was a few days without any conversation, so the company gladdened my usually reclusive heart. The couple effused amiable enthusiasm for outdoor activities. I noticed, however, that as I continued to run into them around the campground, they seemed to be made uncomfortable by me. I didn't think this could be the result purely of the backpacking smell I had developed. And although I was a little starved for conversation, I wasn't foisting myself on them either. Yet they were unmistakably avoiding eye contact after the first few encounters. Only after they left the next morning did I deduce the reason.

It was my pants.

Right before hitting the trail I hit up the second-hand store and found what I believed to be the perfect used pants. I should know such things exist only in legend. When will I learn that used pants nearly always have one major problem? Namely, the fly won't stay zipped. Such was the case with these trousers, and the fly not only came unzipped regularly, it gaped broadly when it did so. On top of this, I had somehow failed to notice in the dressing room that the pants were about three sizes too big, thus exposing several inches of underwear. The first couple of times I saw the nice people, I wore a long shirt, hiding these flaws. But the other times, I looked nearly as deranged as I actually am.

Once I reunited with my car, I threw myself into a fling with the great American road trip. The thrumming of the wheels beneath me, the curves of a gravel mountain road, the lonesome wind-abused high plains, the quirky people, the normal people, I love taking the slow route across this country.

Even with stops at national parks and savored visits with friends en route, I arrived at the southern terminus of the Pacific Crest Trail on April 9, four days earlier than anticipated. My friend Scott was flying down to pick up my car on the 13th, so I couldn't get too far ahead of schedule. I decided to complete the first stretch of the trail as day hikes while I waited for him.

Southern California

The southern terminus lies at a dusty intersection of roads running along the U.S. side of the Mexican border, just north of the giant wall that serves little purpose other than to memorialize our own fear. I parked my car in Campo at 5:30 in the morning, one mile from the trailhead. From there, I attempted to pick up the path to follow it south to the border. Local residents and immigrants had worn so many footpaths into the desert that I wasn't quite sure which way to go.

A man on his way into work at the juvenile detention center noticed me wandering around looking confused. He tried to explain the way to get to the trailhead, but he could see that I was getting frustrated, so he glanced at his watch, then said that since he had time before starting his shift he would drop me off. This was the first of what was to be many acts of kindness by strangers who made huge impacts on my trip.

Under the watchful eye of border patrol guards in bullet-proof vests, my benefactor snapped my photo with a disposable camera I have since lost, then climbed back in his SUV. I watched it jostle away before casting around in the half-light for the trail. I don't know if this happens to anyone else, but when a cop is breathing down my neck I tend to assume I have either just done something illegal or am about to. This is probably why, in my flustered state, I forgot to sign the trail register at the trailhead and instead made a beeline for the path. "See, officer? I'm just a harmless little back-packer! I'm not even going to leave a note to say I was here!"

I hiked the dusty mile back to my parked car, then drove to pitch my tent at a county campground farther up the PCT on artificial Lake Morena. The next day, I tackled the 19 miles between Campo and the lake. To do so, I once again drove to Campo and left my car there, intending to take a bus back to it that afternoon.

I loved being up in the hills as the sun rose. Peavey quail reluctantly kept me company and I saw my first horned toad, a creature which resembles a miniature stegosaurus. By 11 a.m. I had 10 easy miles under my belt.

The first good water source came at Hauser Creek. I stopped for lunch in a shady spot occupied by three other hikers—the first I had seen. When they learned that I'm from Wisconsin, one of them asked if there is something called the Kettle Moraine Trail near my home. I replied that no, the trail he was thinking of is called the Ice Age Trail, but that it goes through the Kettle Moraine State Forest. I then patiently explained that kettles and moraines are geologic terms, and I probably even gave some utterly erroneous definition of each word. He listened in apparent interest. Then I asked him about his own background. He looked almost apologetic when he explained that he was, in fact, a geologist.

Upon returning by foot to Lake Morena, I learned that the bus I planned to take back to Campo to retrieve my car only ran two days a week—neither of which was the day I needed it. In spite of the enjoyable day, the hike left me tired, hot, and hungry—and thus not in the best mood for troubleshooting. Once again, a kind stranger noticed me standing around looking despondent and gave me a lift all 20 miles back to my car, refusing any offer of gas money. Two trail angels in two days. For the next five months, I would almost never venture into a town without somebody performing some small or large act of kindness for me. If your faith in humanity is shattered, might I suggest the Pacific Crest Trail?

By the time I picked up Scott at the San Diego airport on April 13th, I had completed about the first 30 miles of trail as day hikes. I developed blisters and a sore Achilles tendon, but otherwise felt sound. Now he and I planned to backpack together a few days before he drove my car up to Oregon for safekeeping.

I first met Scott when we were both college students volunteering at a community kitchen in Bloomington, Indiana. Together we turned donations into nutritious and often delicious meals that were free to all. When he eventually left the upscale restaurant where he worked and applied to work at the kitchen full time, he listed the reason for leaving his previous job as "severe ethical differences with employer." He is a man who likes to feel he can stand behind anything he does, whether it's serving up a meal or one of his infamous puns.

Scott especially stands beside his friends. When Mike died, not many of the people around me knew what to say or do. I was young, my social circle was young. Loss like that wasn't part of many of my friends' experiences. Scott, unfortunately, did know about losing a loved one. No matter how many times I showed up at his door in tears, he welcomed me, fed me, made me feel like I could make it through. Time and again, that's how he's treated me. So you would think I would be nothing but kind to him when he showed up.

I had been juggling so many details about the trip for so long, and now this hand-off of the vehicle was the last major thing to fall into place. I still carried the stress of the planning process with me. Scott and I have been such good friends for the last two decades that I barely censor myself around him at all anymore, so he bore the brunt of my tense mood. Fortunately, he just shook his head and looked perplexed when I got snippy over some small detail. He knew

I'd eventually go back to being the relatively nice human he used to know.

Since Scott himself is virtually without flaws, I like to dwell on those few that he does have. One of which being that he is easily distracted by television. After I picked him up at the airport we spent the night on the town and stayed in a hotel. As I was getting packed up in the morning so we could hit the trail, he pointed out that it was Saturday morning and that Green Lantern was about to air. The only reasonable thing to do, he felt sure I would understand, would be to delay our departure in order to watch it.

He looked at the remote control at the other end of the room.

"No," I said.

"It's a really good show, Gailie."

"I'm sure it is. But we are hiking today."

"We can hike after we watch villains suffer from the glow of the Green Lantern's light." I could understand this, couldn't I?

"No, Scott. We are not going to indulge your imaginary world today."

I've found firmness mixed with a certain amount of condescension to be most effective in these situations, but Scott wasn't relenting. He eyed the remote control, I eyed him. Suddenly, he made a flying leap for the remote, but I was closer so I slithered beneath him to snatch it first. With the device in my grubby little hands, he was still in mid-air and only with a violent twisting of his torso did he manage to avoid slamming his knee into my skull. He lay there with a shocked look for just a moment. "I could have killed you with my knee." He spoke with what I like to think was a sense of horror. But he quickly recovered his composure and truly was horrified to realize that he had lost the battle for the remote.

He lunged again and succeeded in wresting it from my grip. The TV flashed on and while I attempted to kick the back of his legs to cause him to collapse, he began flipping through the channels. Scott is over six feet tall and works out regularly, so my efforts were not as effective as they would have been on a lesser person. I switched tactics, coming around his side and biting his arm while attempting to smash his fingers against a table. (I come from a large, rowdy family.) I got the remote and switched off the TV even as he snatched the device again. The screen again illuminated.

I was about to attempt a new tackling technique which would have surely made him rue the day he'd ever learned Green Lantern's oath, when he suddenly started chuckling.

"Okay, this is just absurd. You win."

Are there any sweeter words in the English language? Two hours later we arrived at the trail.

Leaving the car at a national forest campground, Scott and I first walked south to make up a few miles of trail I hadn't yet hiked. On the return, we took a recommended spur to see Kitchen Creek Falls, the trail for which ended with a nice view of the water at a steep drop-off down to a canyon. After a short break we planned to turn back to the PCT, but an older couple emerged from below. "If you want to see the really pretty part of the falls, you have to descend here," they advised.

The path they had taken looked a bit treacherous, and therefore Scott foamed at the mouth to get down there. I was concerned about aggravating my sore heel and remained above, pretending not to care that I had just been upstaged by a 79-year-old man and his 74-year-old wife.

I waited around for Scott a while, then decided to head back to the campground. Scott hikes faster than I do, so I expected him to catch up any time. I passed the older couple along the way. They asked where my "husband" had gone and when I cheerily explained that I was sure my friend would catch up later, they seemed appalled that I had left him down there by himself. They reminded me that the trail down the canyon was full of loose rocks and steep cliffs. I began to feel guilty, but as I was speaking to them, I remembered that he had my car keys, so I wouldn't be able to set up camp until he arrived. This made me grouchy instead of guilty.

Yet as time went on and I still had no sign of Scott, remorse dogged me. I kept thinking how alarmed the couple had looked when I told them we separated. I knew full well that Scott was perfectly capable of returning from the canyon. It wasn't that treacherous, it just seemed like more than I was up for with a slight injury. Still, I had been hiking a long while and he hadn't caught me. When I got to the junction where the side path rejoined the PCT, I drew an arrow in the dirt along with my initials to make sure he remembered which way camp lay. Surely he would catch me any minute.

The sun sank a little lower in the sky, and still no Scott. He's a man who has survived a lighting strike, brain surgery, a 250-pound weight dropped on his chest, and any number of falls from great heights. Wouldn't it just be my luck to have him croak when it would be my responsibility to drag his corpse out of the mountains? As time continued to elapse I worried and felt ashamed for having been so short with him the last couple days. These feelings manifested themselves in the action of manically drawing ever more arrows accompanied by my initials so that he would be sure to remember which way he needed to go to find camp.

At last, when the campground came into view, I stopped drawing arrows and sat around the car trying not to be annoyed that I couldn't get into it. Predictably enough, Scott was not far behind me. He saw the campground and, at the one and only junction I had left unmarked, he turned too soon and approached a fence rather than the entrance. He was about to prove his superiority to the fence by dismantling it when I derisively hollered that if he were to move to his left about 15 feet, he would find an opening. To this day he remains surprisingly unappreciative of this nugget of wisdom.

That night, a 40-something backpacker set up camp a few sites down from us, from whence we could hear the music blaring out of his MP3 player. He soon introduced himself as Clatter.

Speaking very broadly, two different approaches predominate on the PCT. The traditional approach is to have as much as you need to be reasonably self-sufficient and prepared for a fairly wide range of emergencies. This results in heavy packs and puts you on the receiving end of smirks from people taking the other approach. This other approach is called "ultralight," and suits people who are willing to

Hike Your Own Hike (HYOH)

When I first began long distance hiking, there was an expression: "Each person hikes his own trail." It summed up the beauty of the eccentric hiking community, so full of oddballs with oddball reasons for hiking. Each of us experienced our hikes in our own way, facing our own unique set of fears and being rewarded with our own unique set of joys. This saying reminded us that there was no "right" way to do a long distance hike.

Over time, the expression has changed to "hike your own hike." It is now an almost arrogant form of advice given to newcomers. For example, some less experienced hiker might ask a group of more experienced folks about the gear he or she has planned on taking on the PCT. Instead of trying to help the person figure out what the right gear would be for the type of hiking experience they want, the reply comes, "If I were you I wouldn't want to be lugging around all those heavy clothes, but hey, HYOH."

***

gamble that nothing too terrible will happen to them. With their light packs, they can go farther faster, meaning they have to carry less food and water. It does also mean they are less likely to be injured, since heavy packs contribute to all sorts of calamities. Most ultralight packers would argue that their approach is at least as safe as the traditional style.

For traditional packers like me, one of the most annoying questions to be asked by other hikers is, "What's your base weight?" I really didn't know how much my pack weighed, but I knew it was probably about twice as heavy as that of most ultralighters and I always felt judged by them—or at least I did early in the hike when everyone seemed more inclined to judge one another. By the end everyone just figured everyone else had a style that worked for them.

Nonetheless, I admire the pluck of the ultralight crowd and their sometimes ingenious strategies for saving weight. Rather, I only admire the ones mentally prepared to bear the inconvenience and risk associated with their strategy. A minority of ultralighters, however, have at the core of their strategy the assumption that those of us carrying heavier packs will help them out if they run into problems—which of course we would and sometimes did.

Clatter seemed to have found the sour spot in between ultralight and traditional backpacking, wherein he had lightweight, inadequate gear, yet still carried one of the heaviest packs I've seen. It was full of electronic equipment, heavy clothes, and I'm really not quite sure what else. He didn't carry a tent, which is why during the previous evening's snow storm he had asked some other hikers if he could crawl into their tent with them. They allowed him to squeeze into their vestibule.

Although his loud voice and music were a nuisance, we managed to mostly escape his attention that evening, with him asking nothing more from us than a ride to town (we weren't headed to town so he was out of luck).

Typical Contents of Traditional vs. Ultralight Packs

The division between traditional and ultralight backpacking is not a stark one. Traditional backpackers still try very hard to keep their packs light, and most ultralighters carry a few things that aren't strictly necessary. By the end of the trail, many traditional hikers have thrown out a lot of things they never dreamed they could give up, and many ultralighters have added a few things that they never dreamed they would carry.

Both types of backpackers will normally carry the following: headlamp, sleeping bag (or light-weight down quilt), sleeping bag liner, sleeping pad, camera, water bottles/bladders, food, cellphone, tooth-brush, duct tape, basic first aid, long johns, short-sleeved shirt, light jacket, ground cloth, hat, gators, nail-clippers.

Some items that traditional backpackers often carry which some ultralighters consider luxury items include: tent (though nearly everyone carries at least some basic shelter in rainy Oregon and Washington), rain gear, long pants, fleece shirt, bug spray, bug net, tooth-paste, stove and cook set, water purification device, more extensive first aid, maps, extra socks, extra underwear, town clothes, extra batteries, pocket knife, rope, warm hat and gloves, camp shoes, hiking poles.

***

The next morning, Scott and I donned our backpacks and headed north to Mount Laguna—which had been the recipient of most of the aforementioned snow. I am a traditional backpacker, whereas Scott is—well, he's just insane regarding how much weight he is willing to carry. Only by calling upon my most potent reservoir of ridicule was I able to persuade him to leave his 22-inch machete behind.

Along the way, we leap-frogged Clatter a few times and got to see him in action. As he explained at length, he was allergic to sunlight, which is why he wore a flap of cloth tied around his nose, a hat with bandanas on either side, and a fluorescent heavy long-sleeved shirt (though the reason he glued fringes to it was so that if he fell off a cliff, his body would be recognizable as the only one who wore a fringed neon-yellow shirt). Additionally, he wore huge knee-length rattlesnake-proof gators. For all these precautions, he gave the impression of someone who hadn't really thought things through. At one point we found him sitting by the side of the trail looking sad. He told us he had been trying to get the last bit of freeze-dried mango out of his snack bag. As he tipped it toward his mouth he accidentally inhaled a snoutful of freeze-dried mango dust, which was now reconstituting itself in his nasal passageways.

The trail astounded, taking us up out of the desert and into the snowy evergreens, where the air smelled crisp and wholesome. We found edible pineapple weed and also gave a nibble to live oak acorns just to see how they would taste raw—unsurprisingly they were acrid. Along the way we came across tracks we assumed were made by someone wearing those "barefoot" shoes, though I later found out that in fact the tracks were made by a man who had experienced some sort of boot calamity and was actually hiking barefoot with a full pack through the snow. I hope that he is somewhere writing a book of his own right now.

We camped atop Mount Laguna at around 6,000 feet. The following morning we attempted to visit a small store nearby, but found it closed. I like things to fall into place, but usually I am pretty able to roll with the punches. For the last few weeks, however, I had found myself knocked off-kilter fairly easily. When I saw that the store was closed, I let off a torrent of complaints that induced Scott to offer up almost all his remaining food. He was turning back to the car that day to start his long road trip home to Oregon, so he only needed snacks for his hike back down the mountain. Even so, he was parting with some premium and pricey snacks on my behalf.

To say I was sorry to see Scott go would be an understatement. How many people have a friend who will fly down to meet them, knowing the experience will be filled with abuse and ridicule, and then take a 21-year-old car with 220,000 miles back across the country to take care of it for a summer? (Actually, Scott's girlfriend Meghan was the real caretaker and deserves the credit for that, but Scott would have been the one to receive the blame from me if things had gone badly.) I hope that each of you reading this has just such a friend, though I'm certain that there are none quite like Scott anywhere.

I was all the more sorry he wasn't with me that day because the landscape only grew more intriguing. Walking along the spine of the Lagunas, I had my first view of the Desert Divide. The mountains trap moisture on the west side, creating a rain shadow on the east. From the high ridges, I could look to the west and see the relatively green hills covered in manzanita, mountain lilacs, and occasional clusters of trees. On the east rain-shadowed side, however, lay the Anza-Borrego Desert—as desolate and brown a place as I've ever seen. Not having looked very far ahead on my maps, I felt foolishly happy that—however hot I was already—at least I wasn't going down there.

This day held other adventures. Surprisingly enough, in all the hundreds of miles I had logged previously, I had never once seen a rattler. Here was my first, stretched lazily across the trail. I thought it would slither away upon my approach, but instead it just looked at me and flicked its tongue. From a distance, I pitched a few pebbles at it to try to get it to move, but it was undaunted. I adjusted one of my hiking poles to its longest setting and attempted to use it to move the snake to the side. Imagine trying to move a rope with a stick when the rope has just enough sentience to resist your efforts. This snake was determined to lie across the trail. I figured if it was that unconcerned about me, I may as well just sidestep it. I gave it as much space as I could on the narrow terrain as I passed. The snake never gave me a second look.

That evening, a number of other hikers and I ended up at a picnic area where camping was technically prohibited. A local advised us that the rangers might look the other way for PCT hikers as long as we didn't set up our tents until after dark. Since water was scarce after this picnic area, I was among those deciding to stay. Clatter grasped the fact that we shouldn't set up tents until sunset, but failed to appreciate that the larger point was to not give the picnic area a camped-in feel. It was one thing to allow thru-hikers to set up a brief camp as we passed through during the short period of April when we were common, but rangers wanted to

WHY SO MANY HIKERS?

My friend Portrait referred to 2012 as the Golden Year of the PCT, and I don't disagree. The year before had been a record snow year. Even people waiting until late June to enter the High Sierras encountered snow so deep that they were constantly in danger of losing their way. Some broke ribs or blew out their knees making the passage. Others were slowed to such an extent that they arrived in town not having eaten for two days. By contrast, I was able to start up into the Sierras the first week of June and encountered very little snow. Almost never was it deeper than my mid-thigh. Most of it didn't even reach my shin. As a result of the snow, many hikers had been unable to complete the trek the previous year, and some came back to start it again. Also many hikers who might have been on the fence about whether to try the hike were swayed by the low snow levels to go ahead and give it a try. On top of this, backpacking is simply growing in popularity and seemed a good option to people with a little bit of means but no immediate job prospects in the slow economy.

***

discourage the location from developing the wear and tear of a full-blown campground.

Clatter spread out all his gear and, of course, blasted his music. He loudly mentioned several times that since he didn't carry a tent, he wouldn't need to worry about the pesky business of waiting until dark to make camp. When newcomers arrived, however, he greeted them with the careful instructions that they were not to pitch their tent yet.

In general, the lack of solitude was to be one of the biggest challenges I faced in Southern California. Nearly twice as many hikers as usual had embarked on the trail as had in previous years, and few had yet dropped out. Even with some of the hikers that I truly came to enjoy, I often felt hemmed in. The first few hundred miles of trail presented only sporadic water sources, and we bunched together to camp near them. More experienced hikers tended to sleep away from water sources in order to avoid the crowd, but the parching unfamiliarity of the desert anchored me to water sources in the early days.

With all the other hikers around, different styles would inevitably come into conflict. I always had the idea that backpackers should try to leave as little impact as possible, and that concern for conservation should in part dictate decisions such as where to pitch a tent, how to wash clothes or dishes (or oneself), and whether to build a fire. But many PCT hikers were either unaware or unconcerned about their impact on the environment, and this was to be a constant source of frustration for me, though also an opportunity for me to attempt to be a little less holier-than-thou (not an easy task, as anyone who knows me will tell you).

I recall one example of hikers who were great people, but a bit oblivious in some ways. These experienced backpackers were generally environmentally aware. Thus they surprised me when they set up their stove in the middle of some dry grass. Trying not to sound overbearing, I gently suggested that perhaps instead of placing the stove on grass, they would like to use one of the many flat rocks nearby. "Oh, it's okay," replied the man as he lit a match, "we took a fire safety course." Once the stove was lit, he realized what he had done and began frantically pulling up the grass from all around the flame, while I edged toward the nearby creek. As he stamped out a few burning patches, he swore he would never make that mistake again.

You may recall the brown, barren rain-shadowed land I saw from the spine of the Laguna Mountains. A couple days of hiking brought me unsuspectingly down to the very floor of that Anza-Borrego Desert. Here I had the thrill of seeing my first scorpion, but what I remember most is the unrelenting heat as I hauled myself across that shade-less, mois-

A BACKPACKER'S IMPACT

As a person hikes along by herself or in a small group, it's easy to imagine that individual acts of small abuse of the ecosystem don't particularly matter. Long distance hikers seem particularly vulnerable to a mindset lacking proper care for the wilderness. We travel fairly quickly, and are unlikely to return. So we don't see the still-stunted growth where we pitched our tent on fragile vegetation a year earlier. We don't see the impacts of smoldering fires left behind, which only ignite later. We don't connect a decision to lather and rinse in a lake with the pollution that laps up on the shores later. (You shouldn't even use biodegradable soap in lakes or streams. If you are going to use soap of any kind, the only responsible way to do it is to carry water away from the shore for washing.) If I could change one thing about the culture of long distance hiking, it would be to instill a greater sense of respect for the ecosystems that host us.

***

ture-less, dust-covered trail. By 11 a.m. the sun had extracted the last of my energy, so it was lucky the trail passed near a bridge that provided relief from the sun. Better still, trail angels had adopted this spot and kept it stocked with water.

A water cache lay under a tarp behind a tree. The large canister carried a sign asking users to call a certain number when the level fell below a painted line, which it had. Muttering the number over and over to myself for memorization, I started to cross the road to return to my pack and fish out my phone. A motorcyclist saw me crossing and stopped to say hello.

"Are you hiking the Pacific Crest Trail?" I responded in the affirmative. After preliminary chatting, he began explaining what I would need to make the journey. For some reason, non-backpackers often assume that those of us doing long trails are completely stumped as to what we should pack, and they are ready to give us plenty of advice! "I've done a lot of motorcycle trips, so I can tell you what you need." He urged me to get a gun, a multi-function tool like a Leatherman, and cotton balls soaked in petroleum jelly (for starting fires).

If you have not been backpacking much, these might seem like reasonable suggestions, so I'll take a minute to explain why I carried none of them. Primarily, the weight is too much to justify. Moreover, I wouldn't have had much use for any of them. I am a terrible shot, and in the extremely unlikely event someone or something attacked me, it's hard to imagine having time to fish the gun out of my pack, get a good sight lined up, and do anything other than blow off one of my own body parts. As for the multi-use tools, those are great for road trips, but the only metal tools I need on a hike are a knife, nail clippers, and a needle—a slim can opener could be justifiable weight too. And in the entire 2,670 miles of the Pacific Crest Trail, I never personally started a fire. I did carry matches and a lighter in case of emergency, but campfires aren't part of the backpacking experience for me. If I want to cook, I simply take a small stove. Throughout most of the trail, building fires is pretty irresponsible due to the risk of it running out of control in the arid landscape.

I knew this man was trying to be nice by offering up these suggestions, so I listened politely and thanked him for his advice. By this time, I had clean forgotten the phone number to call, so I asked if he had a cell phone and whether he would be willing to come the few yards back to the tank to find the phone number and call it. "What kind of water tank?" He asked suspiciously. "For the illegals?"

No, this tank was for hikers, and I told him so. But regardless of one's beliefs about immigration, I mourn the fact that so many of my fellow citizens have reached a point that they would rather see people die a horrible death of thirst in the desert than permit them a drink of water. I used to think the old-timers were oversimplifying the problems of the world when they pulled out the cliché that "all the trouble boils down to man's inhumanity to man." As I get older myself, however, I think there is a lot of truth to that.

In any case, the motorcyclist did call the number to let the trail angel know the water supply was too low and I returned to the shelter of the bridge. All too soon, I was joined by Clatter and a few other hikers. Clatter, by the way, is really not a bad guy, just a very annoying one—with a theater-trained voice which he uses incessantly. Two of the other hikers were also at the garrulous end of the personality spectrum. Determined to take a nap through the hottest part of the day, I announced that we would now be having quiet time. They blinked at me, but spoke not another word.

I unrolled my sleeping pad and lay down. I hadn't closed my eyes 10 minutes when another hiker started shouting, "Hey! Hey! Hey!" I grouchily opened one eye, but when he suddenly remembered my name and exclaimed, "Gail! Gail!" that got my attention. I sat bolt upright just as a very large diamondback rattler stopped in its tracks on the route it had been taking directly toward me. It coiled itself about 12 feet away and there it stayed.

So far as I could tell, it didn't plan to do anything menacing. Like us, it was just trying to get out of the sun. I watched it from the corner of my eye. The jolt of adrenaline had de-

TRAILNAMES

I'm not sure how the tradition started, but on at least three of the long trails in the United States—the Appalachian, Pacific Crest, and Continental Divide Trails—nearly all thru-hikers and many section hikers end up with a nickname. (A thru-hiker is one who is attempting the entire hike in one season, a section hiker is just doing a portion.)

Usually, a name is bestowed by fellow hikers, but sometimes people choose one for themselves. Names people give themselves are often romantic and nature-based such as "Running Wolf" or "Sunny." Trailnames that are awarded to a hiker can sometimes be based partly on good-natured mockery, such as "BASA," who had gotten lost after somehow managing to miss a Big-Ass Stone Arrow pointing out the trail.

A trailname usually follows a person from one long hike to another. Sometimes hikers try to scrap ones they don't like, but it's not so easy to do. Opus, for example, had never been quite satisfied with the name he used on the Appalachian Trail and hoped a new one would emerge on the PCT. Unfortunately for him, in the very first days out of Campo he fell in with people who had met him on the AT and everyone else took it as a matter of course that his name was simply Opus.

After my hike I found it almost disorienting to connect with people over electronic media and find out that my friends with names like Train, Supergirl, and Memphis actually had perfectly ordinary monikers in real life.

***

railed my plans for slumber, so I pulled out my maps to study them. The arrangement made the other hikers uncomfortable, and they threw rocks at the serpent until it hid in a rock pile. To my dismay, everyone soon chattered away again.

By the end of the afternoon, the group gathered under the bridge included Clatter, two hikers intending to do "only" the first 1,000 miles, a couple from Washington, and Frost—a hiker who got his trailname on the Appalachian Trail. Of those assembled, only Frost and I would complete our goal that year.

The main topic of conversation among us was the various strategies to employ over the course of the next 24 miles through the San Felipe Hills. The hot desert section has a shortage of campsites and lacks natural water sources, though trail angels provide a cache about 12 miles in. Two basic approaches to this stretch emerged. Frost and others decided to set out in the late afternoon and camp a few miles into the hills to hit the cache early in the next day before descending again to Barrel Springs. With the temperature still near 100 degrees, I simply couldn't push myself out into the sun that afternoon. Clatter, the Washington couple, and I all preferred to camp under the bridge and rise before the sun to start the hike and then camp near the water cache.

We planned to rise by 3 a.m. and start hiking by 4. Instead, we rose at 4 and I set out about 5 just behind the couple and just ahead of Clatter—who had managed to spill about half a gallon of water into his pack.

The sun hadn't yet risen, and what little moon there had been was already set. The sky held an array of stars and I rather hated to diminish them by turning on my headlamp. I tried to leave it off when the terrain was fairly level so I could enjoy the predawn in its natural beauty. But when I started hearing the sounds of something moving ahead of me, I got a little nervous and shined my light around. Cougar sightings in this part of the country are not terribly uncommon, and I had already spoken to one hiker who had seen one. I recognized, of course, that if a cougar were stalking me I would not be likely to hear a thing, but still I thought it couldn't hurt to use my light. As it happened, the noise was simply the echoes of the footsteps of the two hikers who had set out before me. Their sound rattled eerily far from their bodies in the series of cliffs and side canyons.

I later learned from another hiker that he had seen two cougar cubs while night-hiking this stretch. He never did catch sight of the mother, a fact which rendered him both relieved and unsettled.

As soon as the sun rose, the San Felipes lived up to their reputation as a sun-baked, difficult climb. But I also found it quite beautiful, with good views once again of the startlingly barren Anza-Borrego hemmed in by the red mountains I had descended the previous morning. Most people break the San Felipes into two days, but when I reached the water cache, I took one liter and decided to press on. I thought I would find some small campsite along the 12-mile descent to Barrel Springs. I also thought that by pushing on, I might put Clatter behind me.

My frustration with Clatter was out of proportion to problems he created. However, I require more solitude than anyone else I have ever met, and prior to the trail I had arranged my life in such a way that I could get it. I lived alone. I worked remotely from my home. I only saw people on those occasions that I drove to town for supplies or the very occasional social outing. I knew that the PCT would probably be populated enough, at least at first, to require social effort, but I hadn't expected to be absolutely inundated with company—or to encounter people who were so chatty. So, while Clatter drove many people nuts, he put an especially heavy burden on my psyche because I am especially solitary.

As I strode through the San Felipe Hills, I caught a second wind. In spite of the heat, I suddenly felt I could walk forever. I passed up one campsite after another and eventually realized that I may as well go all the way to Barrel Springs. This would make a 24-mile day, which at the time was the farthest I had ever hiked in a single stretch. I was sure to get ahead of Clatter now.

Not many people chose to hike through the heat of the afternoon, so I mostly had the trail to myself and I felt great for some time. Then, just as my aching feet threatened to bring down my mood, an arrangement of rocks caught my eye. Someone had used them to write out the number 100. This marked my 100th mile on the PCT! I hadn't been keeping close track of my mileage, so this surprise couldn't have left me more ebullient.

Still riding high, I traipsed into the Barrel Springs campground. I could make out the figures of three other hikers already assembled around an unlit campfire ring. One of them hollered out to let me know a trail angel had come by with some pop and chips, pointing to the stash upon which I gleefully descended without another glance at the humans. One of them called out to me, "Hey, Gail, I hiked 24 miles today too! That's a personal record!"

I had bruised my heels badly in the course of the day, and I couldn't push on any farther so there was nothing to do but holler back with as much cheer as I could muster, "Hi Clatter, how ya doing?"

It was time for resupply. I rose that morning to head into Warner Springs. This small town used to have a resort that was an important resupply point for hikers, but it had closed abruptly a few weeks earlier. Some of the townspeople were concerned that hikers would show up needing supplies and not be able to get them. So they quickly put together a fantastic little store in their community center. Volunteers staffed it daily and donated all the proceeds to the school district (which had been dependent on the property tax from the resort).

These people treated us like royalty. They served hot meals, set up an internet station, and even let me borrow a bucket so I could wash out my clothes. Here I was able to get the food I needed to last me until I picked up a package I had shipped to myself 50 miles farther up the trail.

I was also able to purchase some bandages for a unique problem caused by my boots. In addition to the usual blisters so many hikers suffered, the tongue of my boot had rubbed raw a spot where the ankle meets the shin. Although it hurt very little when I walked, minor infection had set in. One of the volunteers found the sight so alarming that he urged me to stay the night with him and his wife while

TYPICAL FOOD

Many people ask what I ate on the trail and expect an interesting answer. They may be disappointed by my reply, but no one is sorrier than me to report that the backpacking diet is altogether mundane. Up until about mile 800, I carried a small stove, and my diet usually consisted of the following:

Breakfast: 3 granola bars and a power shake.
Lunch: Tuna or peanut butter and crackers.
Supper: Ramen noodles, or instant pasta or rice dinners.
Snacks: Nuts, energy bars.

I'm afraid this pretty much concludes the list of the things that comprised my caloric intake.

***

I let the sores soak up the antibiotic ointment. My decision to continue hiking that day represented perhaps the only time in my trek that I turned down an offer of hospitality. I felt these people had already done more than enough to help me out. Also, Clatter planned to spend the night on the lawn there, so I wanted to try to push ahead of him.

In late afternoon I felt as refreshed as a person who hasn't showered in a long time can feel. I set out across the pastureland surrounding the small town. In places, belligerent bovines blocked the path, but with the wide, flat terrain it proved no problem to go around them. I always laugh when I run into cows because they do intimidate me and I have to remind myself that they are pretty clueless about the size differential between us.

The next couple of days exposed me to some of the worst heat yet. Having lived in the Upper Midwest for the last eight years, I had grown used to mild summers where the sunlight gently kisses one's cheeks and a gentle breeze brushes the abundant greenery. In Southern California, the furnace of a sun, the brown earth, the scraggy chaparral, and the dust all conspired to wear me down both physically and mentally.

Because water is so heavy (roughly 2.2 pounds per liter), the temptation is always to carry as little as possible. I wasn't drinking enough. My urine had developed a red tint that is an early sign of dehydration. I therefore forced myself to carry more water. The extra weight did nothing to relieve the pain in my bruised heels, the huge blisters forming on the backs and sides of my feet, or—most debilitating of all—the sun-induced sense of despair. Each day, as the mercury climbed I became unaccountably forlorn. And as cool evening set in, I became content. The experience convinced me I should never live year-round in the desert.

I found myself slogging up yet another brown mountain in a morning that had already pushed the temperature to 100 degrees when I encountered a sight so beautiful I could scarcely believe it. Where the PCT intersected a dusty gravel road, a small sign informed hikers that Trail Angel Mike was just up the road and we were welcome to get water, sit in the shade, and relax. Shade! I read the word several times, scarcely allowing myself to believe.

I staggered in the direction the sign pointed. I met an on-coming couple who, through thick French accents, expressed their amazement and gratitude for Trail Angel Mike. I soon found myself on a shady porch at an off-grid home. Mike had barbequed earlier in the day and he offered me a beer to go with a drumstick. I had caught him just before he was taking off for his full time home in Los Angeles, but he told me to stay as long as I liked in a parked RV or in a shed he had converted to a hiker shelter.

I took a much-needed rest there and also took stock of my options. Unlike most hikers on the PCT, I struggled often with the urge to quit. When I set out to start the trail, I never really committed to the idea of finishing it. I figured there were too many variables to predict whether I would make it and didn't want to feel like a loser if I had to stop. I told everyone not to expect much from my attempt. Still, I hadn't foreseen being plagued by quite so many doubts nor feeling so defeated in the first 200 miles. I love the lush wooded hills, rivers, and lakes of my Wisconsin home and I kept wonder-ing why I was forcing myself through this desert with its un-familiar flora and decimating heat when I could be paddling my canoe through the Boundary Waters or hiking along the shore of Lake Superior instead. Each day as I forced myself through yet more manzanita, I dreamed of the wild leeks and marsh marigolds just emerging in the Wisconsin spring back home. I still had 600 miles of desert to go. Was it worth it?

Moreover, the company of so many other hikers was crushing my spirit. I found myself in the worst of two worlds: I lacked the solitude that I crave and was unable to make the best of it by striking up friendships with my companions. The majority of PCT hikers are males in their 20s. The next biggest demographic consists of males in their 50s and 60s. As a woman about to turn 40, I had a difficult time relating to the others, and indeed most of the other hikers more or less ignored me.

It wasn't just a difference in demographics, however. In the nearly 20 years since I had begun backpacking, this pastime had changed from a form of recreation favored by naturalists and eccentrics to a sport practiced by people interested in testing their physical limits. In general, during those early days of the PCT, I rarely found other hikers to be particularly interested in the plants or geology. Also in those early days of the hike, I wasn't that interested in testing my endurance as many of them were. Other hikers were invariably nice to me, but we didn't connect.

I made a firm decision while I was at Trail Angel Mike's that when I got to the next road (roughly 30 miles up the trail), I would quit the PCT and return to my beloved northwoods home.

That night, I was alone in Mike's RV when a terrific wind kicked up. I knew that heavy snow was on its way, but not forecast to begin for another couple of days. As I watched clouds billowing in over the mountaintops, I worried that the storm was arriving early and I would be stuck at Mike's. This in itself would not be a bad fate, as it was a perfectly safe place to ride out the weather. The problem was that in two days I was scheduled to check in with my good friend Jessica (the same woman I had lived with in Wisconsin). She had taken on the responsibility of being my point person and figuring out what to do if I didn't arrive somewhere on schedule. With her training as an EMT, her own frequent outdoor excursions, and her role as a member of the local search and rescue team, she was well-equipped with the good sense needed to take on this role. But if I holed up at Mike's for too long instead of checking in, I feared she would have the dogs out looking for me.

The storm shook the RV. Although it produced no precipitation, the dust blew so thickly that it blotted out the stars. The raging wind prevented sleep. I don't know how it is for other people, but the thrill of nature in a pique invariably lifts my spirits. I recall a night on a different trip when the lighting struck all around the mountain. I felt somewhat secure as I was tucked into a ring of trees—until one of them came crashing down not five yards from my tent! I was terrified, yet exhilarated. I would love to spend another night that way sometime. So when the storm at Trail Angel Mike's finally broke around 3 a.m., the calm divided my mind between relief and disappointment.

At 5, I stepped out of the RV into one of the most gorgeous mornings I had seen. The cool air played host to an expansive sunrise. I couldn't help but exclaim out loud, "What a beautiful way to start the day!" Embarrassment struck a few moments later when another hiker emerged from the adjacent shed. I hadn't heard him come in during the storm. He pretended not to notice that I had just been talking to myself.

Every now and then in life, we encounter just the right people at just the right time. This hiker's name was Don't Panic, and he was headed south to Lake Morena for the big PCT kickoff event at the end of April. (Most hikers start around the end of April, so this event is timed for them.) He had hiked the trail twice before and, as his name implied, he exuded calm. He sensed my doubts and as we walked together back to the trail, he assured me that there was really nothing to fret over. He listed off all the things most people worry about: Fuller Ridge in the San Jacintos; Antelope Valley in the Mojave Desert; the high passes in the Sierras. He told me not to fret over any of it.

In fact, I hadn't actually planned my trip well enough to know that I should worry over those particular things, but since they seemed more monumental than the things that were plaguing my nerves, I felt comforted. By the time we parted ways at the trail, I heading north and he heading south, I was no longer hiking toward the highway to get off the trail, but rather was once more en route to Canada.

Two mornings later, I arrived at Paradise Valley Cafe on Highway 74, just ahead of the predicted snowstorm. This café not only serves outstanding food, but accepts parcels sent to PCT hikers. Every time someone walks in the door, the owner exclaims, "Welcome to Paradise!"

The restaurant held a large number of hikers, most of whom I believe I had met previously, but I couldn't be sure. I have a problem known as prosopagnosia, or face blindness. It essentially means that I don't recognize faces. In general this is not a huge problem for me, as I instead recognize people by their voices, gaits, body types, or other distinguishing characteristics. But on the PCT, even people who don't suffer from prosopagnosia struggled to recognize each other. Roughly 70 percent of hikers could be described thus: young white guy, thin, medium height, beard. Virtually everyone had similar gaits, similar body types, similar clothes, even similar patterns to their speech. The result was that I always felt extremely hesitant to engage because I was never sure whether I should be giving someone a warm greeting based on prior acquaintance or if I should be introducing myself. The hesitation I projected doubtless reflected back to me in other hikers' reluctance to draw me into their own circles.

One hiker sat alone at the counter, an older man studiously ignoring the younger crowd. I tried my best to engage with the youngsters, since they seemed up-to-date on the weather. The San Jacinto Mountains lay just ahead and none of us were eager to be caught in a snowstorm.

In May of 2005, an ultralight thru-hiker with decades of hiking experience had died up there in a sudden whiteout. With no map or adequate shelter, he was unable to find his way out or safely weather the storm. A year after his disappearance, two other lost and freezing hikers found his gear and used it to save their own lives. He had kept a journal up to the end, and it told a story of a man who knew his life was finished—as these two hikers' lives might also have been if not for his gear. So I wanted to know what the meteorologists had to say about likely conditions up on Mount San Jacinto.

These hikers were all choosing to hitchhike into the town of Idyllwild to wait out the storm. After enormous breakfasts, they left en masse, leaving just me and the older fellow. I decided I would also hitchhike into town. On my way out, I stopped to offer him some of the extra items from the food parcel I had picked up here. He introduced himself as Lone Wolf and, in turn, offered me his surplus. I scored a couple power bars and in the conversation that followed he suggested we hitch to town together. Neither of us had put out a thumb in some years and were both a bit nervous. He figured he'd have more luck catching a ride if a woman were with him and I figured I'd have less chance of getting picked up by a low character if a man were with me.

We gained encouragement from the fact that every last hiker from the large group had been picked up within 15 minutes. After 45 minutes of giving it our best, however, Lone Wolf and I were starting to feel pretty second-rate. Just as despondency nearly set in, a car going the opposite direction pulled over and urged us to get in. We explained that we needed to go 20 miles in the direction from which the driver had just come, but he said it was no problem.

This man had come from Ireland to try the PCT, but found that any hiking above 4,000 feet left him feeling ill. Experts claim that altitude sickness doesn't affect people until at least 8,000 feet, but I am not going to argue with this man's own personal experience. He decided to leave the trail and planned to do a motor tour of the United States instead. But first, he rented a car specifically to ferry hikers out of the upcoming storm. He refused to accept any gas money when he dropped us off at a hotel. I wish I had gotten his contact information to find out how his journey went.

The unexpected kindnesses continued over the next couple days. I registered at the Idyllwild Inn, feeling a bit nervous about spending money for a hotel that hadn't been in my budget. When I gave the clerk my credit card, she informed me that my room was already paid for, so the card would just be for incidentals. I gaped. Who had paid my room? It turned out that a PCT hiker had just been through and had planned to stay two nights. Instead, he left after only one night and asked her to give the room to the next hiker who came along—which was me.

Up until now I had been trying to record all the random kindnesses shown to me by strangers. I had vowed that when I returned I would perform at least as many random acts of kindness myself. However, the sheer number had already become difficult to track and I began to realize that I could not repay them by some tit for tat method. Rather, the key was to become the sort of person who would go out of my way to help other people achieve their dreams. I try to train myself now to break through my customary solitary manners to offer a hand to friends and strangers alike. I had so many good examples of this sort of behavior on the PCT that I believe some of it may have rubbed off on me.

I ended up staying three days and two nights in Idyllwild while a storm visibly raged thousands of feet above. I made good use of my time to send some gear home and replace other gear.

I also got to know my neighbor at the hotel. Matt, a returned veteran from Afghanistan, is from Kansas and was about to embark on 400 miles with his mountain bike. Idyllwild's many fine restaurants beckoned, but I resisted their lure. Matt noticed me miserably forcing macaroni and cheese down my gullet on my second evening in town. Taking pity, he convinced me it that it would be a much better idea to let him take me to dinner. I hung out with the biker crowd that night and they quite impressed me. Although these athletes were all about to compete with each other, they expressed nothing but support for one another.

GEAR CHANGES AT IDYLLWILD

With about 150 miles under my belt, I switched up my gear a little for better performance and lighter weight. I made the following purchases in Idyllwild.

- New cook set (smaller and titanium)
- Light-weight parasol to help shield the sun
- Water purification tablets to replace my filter
- Tank top and light-weight long-sleeved shirt to replace cotton shirts (I wondered for the next 2,000 miles why the long-sleeved shirt always seemed tight around the chest—but when I had tried it on, Wolf had assured me it looked just fine, that dog. Shortly before I reached Canada I realized I had purchased a man's shirt.)
- Single-blade knife
- Microspikes to help me keep my grip on snow and ice

I also sent home the following items:

- Gators (Most hikers use them to keep out dust and stones, but I found them not worth the extra heat they trapped.)
- Sleeping bag liner (I regretted this decision when my bag became filthy and later had the liner shipped back to me.)
- Water filter
- Stainless steel cook set
- Cotton long-sleeved shirt
- Two cotton t-shirts
- Knife with attachments

Altogether I was able to lighten my load by about two pounds.

***

Most of the bikers were men, but one woman gave a very friendly wave as I entered. I waved back and smiled. After her meal, she approached our table and introduced herself. She seemed so excited to meet me, but I couldn't think of very much to say beyond warmly wishing her best of luck. Later I caught sight of another mountain biker—a fairly famous one—who bore a slight resemblance to me (though she is about eight times as hot as I am). It then dawned on me that the woman in the restaurant probably thought I was her and I even suspect the two may have communicated in some way previously, which would explain why she had seemed so expectant when she introduced herself.

Sometimes passionate hikers and passionate bikers can end up feeling a little friction. Since bikers aren't allowed on the Pacific Crest Trail, they ruefully refer to the PCT as the Perfect Cycling Trail. This may change, as a group of bikers has asked the U.S. Forest Service to reconsider the prohibition against bicycles on the PCT. I must say it would significantly detract from the hiking experience to share the trail with high-speed wheeled vehicles, but mostly I am just amazed that anyone would willingly hurl themselves down those steep trails on a bike. Clearly, I am not cut out for the sport.

In spite of all the rest and good luck I found in Idyllwild, my nerves still jittered as I contemplated the trail ahead. The next leg of the journey would take me into the now snow-covered San Jacinto Mountains. Just before descending out of them, I would have to traverse Fuller Ridge, notorious for its hazardous and icy conditions. With all the fresh snow that lay ahead, I once more struggled with self-doubt. But when I went to the library to check email, I found my inbox full of supportive notes from friends and family. I had no idea how excited my loved ones would be about this hike. Everyone expressed complete confidence in me, and I allowed their faith to take the place of my insecurity.

Before setting out for the trail, I stopped in for breakfast at a local diner. Lone Wolf sat at the counter and I sidled up next to him. We agreed to hitch together back to Paradise

Valley Café. From there we decided to tackle the San Jacinto Mountains jointly.

Lone Wolf (or just Wolf, as I called him when I was with him in the interest of accuracy) is an interesting guy. He retired after 37 years of highway maintenance, but still had some debts from his kids' college bills. So, with no previous nautical experience, he took up a second career as a sailor. Now he was fully retired and attempting his first really long hike. His solitary nature matched well with my own so that we were able to keep each other company without grating on each other's nerves.

The first stretch up into the San Jacintos presented long dry miles. Our maps informed us that our only options to replenish water bottles lay off trail down steep descents. We opted to draw from Eagle Springs, only a quarter mile from the path. Leaving our packs at the top, we picked our way down the side of the mountain. Upon arrival, we found the spring was not running so much as dripping. Somewhat fortunately, trail maintainers had built a trough to catch the water. As a result, we had the opportunity to fill our bottles from the brown, stagnant water pooled beneath the outlet. This would have to do.

That night we camped on a bluff with a clear view of the lights of Palm Springs way down in the desert below. Something about the desert air makes the lights shimmer in a peculiar and beautiful way unfamiliar to a Midwesterner like me. It was romantic enough to make me wish I had a lover to watch it with, but nothing like that ever materialized between myself and my new friend.

Snow plants now began pushing up the earth. When these strange pink shoots first emerge, they look for all the world like toy rockets (or, according to some, a certain body part). Later, these chlorophyll-less plants develop dainty little flowers, all the while getting their nutrients via a relation-ship with fungi.

In spite of the presence of snow plants, those first cou-ple of days in the mountains we didn't actually have to con-tend with much of their namesake. But once we rose above 7,000 feet, we often could do little better than follow others' footsteps and hope those who laid them had kept more or less on trail. We were probably about the 7th and 8th set of footprints out there. At one point we wandered fairly far off trail, but ran into a local who knew the area backward and forward. He was headed a different direction, but assured us our navigation was basically sound and that we would get back on trail soon. Later we again lost our way, but using map and compass we wound our way back a second time.

At this point we were above 8,000 feet and the altitude brought me fatigue and labored breathing. Only about 20 percent of people suffer from altitude-related problems at such low levels, and I guess I'm just one of the fortunate few. This concerned me because the next day we would have to tackle Fuller Ridge, on the northern slope of Mount San Jacinto. I hoped that after a good night's sleep, the altitude wouldn't trouble me quite as much.

That sleep was not quite as sound as it might have been, however. Wolf and I camped at one of the last flat spots for 20 miles. Toward late evening Neil, Tanya, and Gutsy Rabbit joined us. The first two are a British couple whose wit and obvious enjoyment of each other's company made everyone else enjoy their company as well. Rabbit is a stunning and shy young woman who had already completed the Appa-lachian Trail by the time she was 19. No one ever doubted that she would easily make Canada on the PCT. As much as everyone considered her presence a boon to any group, her real claim to fame was not her own accomplishments, but those of her pet mouse, Ella. The rodent had already joined her on a bike trip across the country and would later become the first mouse to climb Mount Whitney (though the poor thing became dangerously hypothermic at the summit). Rabbit carried Ella in a small shaded cage at the top of her pack.

We all settled amiably into camp. Around dusk, I heard a strange buzzing noise. "Guys, what's that noise?"

Everyone quieted for a moment. "It's a chickadee," replied Tanya.

"No, no, not the bird. It's a strange insect-like sound." They quieted again, but no one else heard a thing.

"There it is again! It's like a bee with a bugle!"

As much as everyone declared they would like to hear such a thing, none of them could. "There! Can you hear it now?" I would exclaim when it was particularly audible. But no. I feared these folks would edge away from me if I persisted in my claim.

The noise went away after dark, then started up again around 3 in the morning—louder and clearer. Clear enough to realize that I had set my tent on top of a bees' nest. I'm not sure why they would have started buzzing again since they aren't usually nocturnal. Maybe it was the warmth of my body, or maybe I had done something to cause them serious distress. I relocated my tent and the sound stopped. The feeling of vindication outweighed any irritation at being wakened in the wee hours.

A light snow fell overnight, collecting on our tents. In the morning my fingers numbed while breaking camp, but once we started moving I felt fine. Fuller Ridge proved to actually be quite easy to traverse, contrary to its reputation. Of course, having fresh snow probably made navigation easier since otherwise we might have been contending with ice. In any case, we were through it in no time.

Having completed the ridge, we made a long, hot, waterless descent over the course of about 18 miles until we found ourselves again on the desert floor. All of our throats parched in the suddenly sun-baked trail that emerged from the high-altitude evergreens. Rabbit got so dry that she had to take some fetid water pooled up shallowly near the trail. The morning's snow drifts seemed to belong to another era.

Upon reaching the bottom of the descent, we were all clean out of water and craving shade. Some entity had, puzzlingly enough, installed a drinking fountain where the land leveled out. An aqueduct pipe ran nearby and we crowded into its meager shadow. When we rested sufficiently, we set out to tackle the final five miles across the desert floor of San Gorgonio Pass, which lay 7,000 feet lower than where we had started that morning.

I expected the flat stretch ahead to be a cakewalk. I hadn't counted on the hot wind blowing sand in such quantity that it obliterated the trail. At times, I had to muster all my strength just to move forward at all through the gusts. Wolf and I kept stopping to reassess our bearings, gradually making our way to the interstate. We knew the trail went under a bridge there.

Some of my slowest miles were the five across the windswept pass. What should have taken less than two hours stretched into three. When we finally shoved ourselves forward enough to reach the bridge under the highway, we were welcomed by the sight of the Brits and Rabbit perched on the concrete footers with—could it be a mirage?—bottles in their hands! Trail angels had left beer and pop! We each picked our poison.

From there we carried on toward the home of those very trail angels. Ziggy and The Bear are the only people I know of who bought their home for the express purpose of being near the trail in order to provide trail magic. Not only do they leave treasure under the bridge, they have a whole system for hosting hikers, feeding them, getting them a shower and whatever else they need. Apparently, this was common knowledge, but I hadn't studied trail culture much before hiking and so I had no idea how big a part of the trail community they were. I was just happy to learn there was a place to stay for the night.

Right before we turned off the trail to follow the signs to their home, a small wooden box stood pathside. A note asked us to sign the register within. When I took the pen, Wolf told me he had been thinking about a potential trailname for me. He had noticed that I tend to sing when I am happy, and for that reason he thought NightinGail would be a good name for me.

With my curmudgeonly ways, I assumed I would never meet someone who would know me well enough to give me a proper trailname, but here Lone Wolf had done it. I accepted his suggestion on the spot.

Five hot and exhausted hikers arrived at Ziggy and The Bear's dusty refuge around sunset. Our hosts gave us foot baths, salad, and ice cream. In case you missed what I wrote in the previous sentence, they gave us foot baths! I was at a loss as to how one even receives such a thing. We were all so overwhelmed by the kindness we didn't even have words. At some point the phrase "thank you" just sounds like a shallow parody of what one actually feels.

The only other hiker there was a young woman named Georgia. Her diminutive 22-year-old frame held a bubbly personality that could give the impression of a bumbler. Never judge a book by its cover. Georgia has a great sense of direction and an unbelievable amount of pluck. She and another hiker named Knut were two of the first hikers across the snow in the San Jacintos and they did an incredible job of pathfinding—much to the benefit of everyone who came after. She was now hiking solo again after Knut had gone into town for resupply.

I had made it through the San Jacinto Mountains. Although originally Wolf and I only talked about hiking together for the few days it took to trek through that range, we decided to continue keeping each other company. The next several nights, we camped with Georgia, the Brits, and Rabbit as well.

Over the subsequent two days, we ascended 7,000 feet into the San Gorgonio Wilderness. The oppressive heat and wind at San Gorgonio Pass had left me in no mood for a climb, but once the first push was behind us, the terrain transformed into one of the most scenic places in all of Southern California, a wide plateau punctuated with sudden canyons. In spite of a lack of water, the plants bore green leaves—actually green, I mean, and not the dull bile-colored tint of most desert foliage.

When the force of the sun diminished the pleasure of the walk, I deployed my new parasol. These are becoming more popular, though still only a minority of hikers carry them. Because the backpacking community is comprised primarily of men who don't like to use the word "parasol," this device is typically called an umbrella. And while it's true that it could also serve to keep off the rain, most people have already sent theirs home before arriving in the rainy sections in the Northwest. The gear is really meant to repel sun. Though I had the facts on my side, the only time Wolf ever got angry with me was when I insisted on referring to his "umbrella" as a parasol.

Forgive me Wolf as I carry on: The most common type of parasol has a reflective silver material on the outside, and is black underneath to diminish glare. On hot days, it significantly reduces the temperature of air adjacent to a hiker's skin. This translates into needing less water, feeling less exhausted, getting less sunburned, and just plain enjoying the hike more. The biggest downside is that when one is accustomed to using hiking poles, it becomes a problem to deploy the parasol as well. At first I put away one of my poles to hold the device, but later I figured out a way to attach it to my pack, though it still required periodic adjustment as I jostled along. Also, strong winds make the parasol virtually impossible to use—though the ingenious design prevents the tool from being ruined by the gusts. I plan to carry mine on any future desert hikes.

In time, we left this hot but glorious San Gorgonio Wilderness for some welcome time in evergreen forests. Up until now, we had not been in bear country. I always hung my food just to keep it away from rodents, but hadn't had to worry about throwing a proper bear hang. In this area, however, people occasionally reported bear sightings, so I gave the matter of my food storage the attention it deserved. I certainly didn't expect to see a bruin, but that night as dusk settled in, we were all crawling into our sleeping bags when I heard a rustling from a clump of manzanita.

I watched the branches thrashing about toward the middle of the clump. I told myself the perpetrator was probably a deer and kept observing. I didn't want to say anything to the other hikers for fear of being laughed at: first a bee with a bugle, now an imaginary bear! But when I saw a hump of black hair rise for a moment above the shrubs, I couldn't help myself. I called out, "Is that a bear?"

Immediately, black-haired Georgia rose out of the manzanita in alarm. "Where?" she exclaimed, looking all around. I burst out laughing. Georgia, who almost never used her tent, was bivouacking among the shrubs.

That was our last night camping together as a group, and except for one brief encounter, I wouldn't see Georgia again for more than 500 miles. Thus a long time elapsed before I discovered that by mistaking her for a bear, I had unknowingly christened her with a trailname that stuck: Little Bear.

An important landmark loomed close now—Big Bear City. From this resort town I would take a series of buses and trains to Los Angeles, where the hospitality of friends Leanna and Hollis awaited.

With proximity to LA came proximity to the movie industry. The PCT runs just a few feet from cages housing predatory animals used in films. After roaming free myself for nearly a month in the wilderness, the sight of grizzly bears pacing the concrete floors of small metal cages did little to improve my opinion of humans and certainly made me question the common disclaimer that "no animals were harmed in the production of this film."

At Highway 18, I said goodbye to my friends and tried in vain to catch a ride into Big Bear City, 5.5 miles up the road, eventually setting out forlornly by foot. It may seem absurd that I am happy to walk 2,670 from Mexico to Canada while being utterly opposed to walking a few miles to a town, but treading on pavement is quite a different experience than hiking through the mountains. Pavement is not only less pleasant scenically, but quite painful on my feet. My weak arches in particular take a pounding on the road while blisters flare from the heat. And blisters were now becoming a serious matter. They were becoming so numerous and so raw that they jeopardized my ability to proceed.

I made my way down the winding shoulder-less highway, listlessly extending a thumb whenever I heard a vehicle approach. I hadn't gone a full mile when a car pulled over and an elderly gentleman offered me a ride. He had never picked up a hitchhiker until two days ago, when he had given a lift to another PCT hiker. This other fellow had been so polite and appreciative that the man decided to give it another go. I hope I left a similarly amiable impression and that the gentleman is still picking up hikers.

After stopping for breakfast I made my way to the town center and from there I boarded a bus to San Bernardino, and then a train to Union Station, where Leanna drove me to her home and treated me to a much-needed rest.

I love cities, and I particularly love Los Angeles. I never would have expected to fall for the metropolis known for its sprawling car culture, its glamorous movie industry, and its money. But when I lived in the area briefly several years ago, I found its vibrancy irresistible.

I had worked for a small independent union in the first years of the century and Leanna oversaw my work. Though my stay in the city of angels was short, we forged a bond that has endured 10 years later. In all that time, I had never been back to LA. Now here I was in one of the world's glitziest cities, arriving in dust-covered clothes that hadn't been changed or washed in a week. The body underneath the clothes reeked similarly. I felt sorry for my fellow passengers and a little embarrassed. Leanna took me right home where I was able to jump in the shower and change into one of her clean t-shirts.

Three mornings later, I still wore the same t-shirt and she asked if I might like a new one. Forgetting that non-hikers would by now probably think I stank a little, I just gave a quick whiff of my pits and shrugged, "Naw."

Leanna and her partner Hollis took everything in stride. After such a long time on the trail without much in-depth conversation, the time with this smart, passionate couple helped ease the loneliness I often felt in Southern California. For although I am a solitary person, I am nonetheless used to being connected with such kindred spirits and loved ones as can tolerate my misanthropic ways. My quirky humor, astute political insights, and ... uh ... I'm trying to think of any other charms I might have ... well whatever they are, they were largely unnoticed and unappreciated by others at this stage of my trip. Even though in the stretch leading up to Big Bear I had hiked with a great crew, I still felt my personality wasn't really coming through. Spending time with Leanna and Hollis boosted my morale immeasurably.

They treated me to more than just good company. I rested in their garden of flowering native plants, ate wonderful food, took in a museum, and even relaxed in front of the TV. I returned to Big Bear City well fed and ready to go. But before I could go on, I needed to replace my boots.

When purchasing gear for the hike, I foolishly bought boots that had a waterproof lining. I had searched in vain for footwear lacking such a lining, but without sufficient perseverance. Most PCT hikers don't wear boots, instead choosing light-weight running shoes in order to let their feet breathe and to keep weight to the minimum. Because I have serious arch problems and because I carry a fairly heavy pack, I worried this option wouldn't give me enough support. What I wanted was a sturdy hiking boot that I could waterproof myself. But for reasons that I don't understand, the major boot manufacturers don't make many models without a waterproof lining anymore.

I never met a PCT hiker who liked these linings. They keep the feet way too hot, even in moderate temperatures. The seams can cause chafing or blisters. In dusty areas, dirt collects between the lining and the exterior, creating lumps that can be excruciating on the toes. On top of all this, they don't actually keep your feet dry. Your feet will be sweat-drenched in good weather, yet the lining doesn't keep out even a light rain.

Blisters are caused by two things: friction and moisture. Hiking my way through Southern California in these boots, I had plenty of both. Whenever I took a break, I removed my boots and socks, all drenched with sweat. Even drying them out as often as I could throughout the day, disaster visited upon my feet. In fact, the needle in my first aid kit had become dull from all the lancing it had to do. Just try lancing blisters with a dull needle and see if you don't develop a choice vocabulary for manufacturers of waterproof linings.

I realized I might not make it much farther if I didn't swap out my footwear. I had looked at a gear store in LA for better boots, but without luck. So now I went to the K-Mart in Big Bear City. There, I picked up some off-brand boots without a waterproof liner and sent my expensive boots home. These new boots ended up lasting me only two weeks before the tread gave out. They also had some kind of flaw that required me to slice away part of the boots' ankle support to prevent them from rubbing away at a tendon. Nonetheless, it was such a relief to have a little air get through. My feet still sweated and I still got blisters, but not on the same scale.

After the boot purchase, I stayed the night at a hostel in Big Bear City. In the morning, the owner offered to drop several of us hikers off at the trail. I was confused when a man wearing a dress shirt and tie loaded into the vehicle with us. At the time Sunny was the only hiker I had seen who wore a tie, though later I met another named, appropriately, Oddball. Sunny was also one of only three deaf hikers I met. Sadly, the most unique impression I have of Sunny is that he was the only thief I met on this or any hike, though that fact didn't surface until later.

As the slowest hiker being unloaded at the trail that morning, I soon enjoyed the freedom of hiking alone again. I missed Wolf, Georgia, Rabbit, and the Brits, but figured I was bound to see them all again sometime if they stopped for some zero mileage days. In the meantime, I shouldered my pack and prepared to find a detour for a section of trail damaged by landslides.

I somehow completely missed the detour and carried on through the main trail. This proved to be a happy accident, as in fact the PCT had been nearly completely repaired. Only one or two somewhat sketchy sections briefly presented themselves on this gorgeous walk high above Deep Creek. Water so rarely manifested itself in Southern California that the sound of it rushing below filled me with joy, even if it was virtually inaccessible at that vertical distance.

The act of staying on the trail also gave me the gift of hot springs! The detour would have caused me to go around them. When I arrived, cool evening air replaced the heat of the day. Perfect time to soak my tired dusty body in hot water! Different springs held different levels of heat. I could sit in a natural hot tub, dunk in the cold creek, then choose another steaming pool. By the end of the night, my body felt better than it had in weeks. All of this good fortune coincided with the day I hit the 300 mile mark, so high spirits accompanied me when I set out again the next morning.

From the Deep Creek hot springs, I headed north toward the Mojave Reservoir, where in a spell of laziness I unthinkingly followed a path I saw hikers ahead of me take. This path proved not to be the PCT. It took some wandering around to get back on course. Such wandering normally wouldn't have been a cause for any particular concern except that my map noted hikers should watch for quicksand in this area.

Quicksand? How does one watch for it? I tried to think of everything I knew about quicksand—and that certainly didn't take long! I think there was an episode of Gilligan's Island once where they got stuck in the stuff. And possibly a Land of the Lost episode too. I believe the victims were urged to stand stock still to keep from getting sucked down farther, but I couldn't recall what form the eventual rescue took. Furthermore, would I have to worry about quicksand even once I found the trail, or could I presume the PCT was mire-free? As far as I was concerned, the map skimped on details.

I carried on without incident toward Silverwood Reservoir, one in a string of artificial lakes tying together the California Aqueduct. With Deep Creek followed by Silverwood, these last 30 miles were the most well-watered days in all of Southern California, and gave me my only two opportunities for swimming in the first 700 miles of trail. (The fact that I

THE AQUEDUCT SYSTEM

Roughly two-thirds of California's population and much of its agricultural industry depend on the hundreds of miles of channels, reservoirs, and pumping stations that make up the aqueduct system. This has allowed the cities of dry Southern California to expand out of fertile valleys and into deserts, while causing problems for people and wildlife upstream. Climate change makes the system vulnerable to the more frequent droughts and rising sea level, which could lead to salinization of all the waterways connected through the system. Many of the structures are vulnerable to earthquakes as well.

When I lived briefly in LA, I naively expected to find a culture very conscious of water's value. To my surprise, I saw less regard for leaking faucets than in the water-rich Midwest and even recall that an outer suburb passed an ordinance forbidding its residents from having brown lawns.

When one considers the far-reaching impact of the aqueduct system on the agricultural products we all consume in vast quantities and on the settlement patterns of this enormous state, it would be difficult to overstate the importance it has played, for good or ill, in shaping our country.

***

chose to swim in Silverwood in spite of signs warning that raw sewage flows into the reservoir shows how desperate I was for ways to cool off.)

What passes for spring in Southern California now raced toward summer. By mid-May, I typically broke camp and hit the trail no later than 5:30 a.m., but within an hour the sun would already make the walking nearly unbearable. Fortunately, every footstep brought me closer to Interstate 15, where just a few hundred yards off the trail the tired hiker can stop in at a fast food restaurant.

SPRING IN THE DESERT

Hiking through the desert in springtime is a privilege conferred on the few. The unpredictable and (for many species) short blooming season make pilgrimages difficult to time. Yet by virtue of walking the desert at various altitudes day after day I witnessed a disorienting variety of flowers, all of which—no matter how isolated—had somehow been found by bees, wasps, and other pollinators. Some, like the sand lupine, I recognized as miniature versions of species found in the lush woodlands of Wisconsin. Others, such as the Seuss-like ocotillo, which shoots up ten-foot stalks that bud and bloom scarlet red and die back all within a few days, required me to ask others to identify. Whenever I saw a local day-hiker, I always inquired of her or him about a few varieties of foliage or birds to add to my knowledge—and the variety of birds amazed me even more than the flowers! I especially enjoyed the Peavey quail and our ability to startle each other.

***

With some chagrin I must report that the approach to I-15 was one of the loveliest stretches in all Southern California. First, the trail followed the rim of razor-like ridges that dropped off steeply on either side. Next, it descended into a serene little canyon housing a merry brook. In spite of this unexpectedly beautiful day, I found myself rushing through, thinking only of what I would order at McDonald's. By 10 a.m. I stood in line surveying the menu.

A law must require fast food establishments to list the caloric content of their meals, because there it all was posted right next to the menu. I usually eat pretty healthy food and don't enter places like this, so I'm not sure how long this has been the case. Using this data point now as my only criterion, I scanned the list to find the highest-calorie meal, then ordered a milkshake-like item to top it off. In this way, I was able to obtain nearly 3,000 calories for under $10. Don't try this at home kids. (Seriously, don't.)

A long dry climb lay ahead, and the day grew to be one of the hottest yet. I felt ashamed to keep my stinky self around non-hikers, but I wasn't about to leave the air conditioned restaurant until the afternoon began to fade. My obstinacy was rewarded when a woman approached to inform me that she had just left a large cache of water at a road crossing five miles up. Her son had nearly completed the trail a few years earlier, so she knew how helpful such acts of kindness could be. Indeed, knowing that water lay ahead saved me nearly 10 pounds of weight I would have carried in my water bottles.

I set out in late afternoon, arriving at the cache as the cooler evening air rolled in. The woman had completely understated what she had done for us. She provided not only water, but cupcakes, juice, and table and chairs! I decided to make camp on the spot. All too soon, the arrival of three hikers broke my solitude: John Wayne, Karate Kid, and Lost.

I settled into my tent to write in my journal. Outside, I heard Karate Kid rummaging around in the dry vegetation half-scorched by some recent fire. I thought at first that he was clearing an area for his own tent, but when I heard something being stacked up a few feet away, I realized with distress that these three hikers were building a bonfire! This might seem like reasonable enough behavior to Midwesterners accustomed to green forests that rarely go up in flames. But in Southern California, we were hiking through one giant tinder box. The dry vegetation, lack of water, and strong hot winds all were virtually designed to assist wild fires. For hundreds of miles we had constantly been walking through large burned-out areas, evidence of what happens when humans are careless with their matches. In this case, my tent was directly downwind from the flame! And when I say downwind, I am talking about violent gusts that whipped our tents.

I asked them to extinguish the flames, but these hikers, who happened to be Israeli, pointed out that there were no signs prohibiting fire. I've noticed that visitors to this country like to make fun of Americans for all of our signs warning of every possible danger. In fact, consistent with our suspicion that people will fail to use good sense at the first opportunity, there had been signs at every major trailhead. Yes, they insisted, but right at this spot there were no signs. True, no printed signs, just natural ones.

I knew it would be useless to argue anymore, but I did resolve to get up and make sure it was out cold after they went to bed. It turns out I needn't have worried about that part. When they were done with the fire, they went to the jugs of water the trail angel lugged in by hand and poured generous amounts over the flames.

A few hundred miles later I learned that one of these guys had cut himself badly in the course of gathering firewood one night and had to go to the emergency room. I am petty enough to have felt some small sense of satisfaction. Soon, however, anyone with a grudge against me would have their own opportunity to feel smug.

The next major climb approached: Mount Baden-Powell, named after Lord Robert Stephenson Smyth Baden-Powell, Chief Scout of the World. He founded the Boy Scouts, and his title has led me to consider founding some organization that would confer a fabulous moniker on me as well. Gail "NightinGail" Marie Francis: Head Pie Maker of the Universe! (I really do make some of the best pies in the universe.) May I have my mountain now, please?

Hikers attain Baden-Powell's 9,400-foot peak via five miles of switchbacks—trail that winds back and forth rather than ascending more directly and vertically. Trail-makers use switchbacks to curb erosion and reduce wear and tear on hikers' knees. Near the top I navigated a few snow-fields, but nothing dangerous. Feeling good but exhausted after the climb, I carried on along a ridge heading west. The trail then descended moderately along a couple more switchbacks. Somehow, at one of these, I switched, but didn't back. Instead I mindlessly followed a little coyote trail that carried on east while the real trail turned sharply west again. Unaware I was on a false path, I encountered a small rock slide and I scampered across, as I sometimes needed to do. Only when I got to the other side, I couldn't pick up the trail again.

The scamper had been more hazardous than anticipated. I didn't feel safe going back across it and I thought I could see where others had carried on ahead, so I did too. But before long, I found myself in a moonscape-like terrain of scree crumbling away with every footstep and with no clear way to maneuver myself out. From some indentations, it seemed to me that some person or creature had taken a descending route that I thought might lead to some kind of gap, from whence I could again ascend. I was about to take that route when I reminded myself that really bad situations are not usually caused by just one or two mistakes, but rather a series of cascading mistakes. With this in mind, I found a stable place where I could sit half-comfortably to rest and assess the situation. I drank some water and pulled out my map and compass to thoroughly orient myself.

Once I understood my true location, I saw that further descent would only increase the danger, and that instead I needed to gain the ridge above. I tried to send a text to my friend Jessica to let her know where I was and to suggest that if she hadn't heard from me again in a few hours she should call for help. Although my phone showed two bars, the screen helpfully informed me it could not connect to the network.

Naturally, I had lost my way on the south-facing side of the mountain, which roasted in the afternoon sun. I tried not to think too deeply about the possibility of falling into the waterless valley below. Instead I focused on picking out a route that seemed most promising. I forced myself to take my time, reminding myself I had plenty of water and daylight. I carefully moved from one stable-looking spot to another. Sometimes a log served as a landing pad, sometimes a boulder served the purpose. In each case, I took care lest I apply too much pressure and cause it to go careening down. After an hour and a half of clambering to within about 300 yards of the top, however, I reached a point where I simply couldn't continue with the backpack on my back. Every time I tried to scramble up, it pulled me back down.

I rested. I re-assessed. When I was certain this wasn't just a case of the sun making me melodramatic and that the pack really was greatly increasing the likelihood of a major accident, I made the decision to leave it behind. I further chose not to think about the implications as I took some water and my money and ID out of the pack. Without an awkward 40-odd pounds strapped to my back, I finished my scramble up the ridge fairly easily.

Not until I crested did I allow myself to feel the import of what I had just done. It was far too dangerous to try to go back down for the pack, and I could never afford to re-equip myself. Nothing to do but to throw in the towel and figure out a way back to Wisconsin. There went the dream of getting to Canada.

I cried all the way back down the mountain.

At this point, I still wasn't totally sure whether I had been off trail, or if the trail had simply eroded. I was pretty sure the fault was mine, but worried other hikers might end up in a similar predicament, so as I descended, I advised the oncoming hikers to be careful. Toward the end of the 4,000-foot descent, I met a young hiker named Caveman. This is the one and only time I met him, but I will remember him the rest of my life for the kindness he showed. While most of the PCTers seemed to (understandably enough) think I was an idiot for getting lost and merely thanked me politely for giving them a few words of warning, Caveman stopped and listened with sympathy. Then, without a moment's hesitation he said, "Come on, I'll help you get your pack back."

I explained that it really wasn't safe to try to get it, but he insisted, "We'll go slowly. I've got rope, we'll figure out a way to do it." When I still hesitated, he urged, "Come on, we can do it!"

So, I began following him back up the mountain. He set a brisk pace, and soon I remembered that I hadn't eaten since 10 that morning. I felt mentally and physically weak. I called out to him and he turned around. "I just can't do it today," I told him.

He nodded sympathetically. "Well, look, go into town and get some rest. In the morning you can find someone else to help you. And if you really can't get the pack back, you can figure out a way to outfit yourself again. Even if it takes you two weeks to get it all worked out, you have plenty of time to get to Canada. Your trip is definitely not over."

Caveman, wherever you are, thank you for being such an incredibly kind and positive person. You saved my hike by infusing me with just a little bit of self-confidence at a time when I couldn't summon it on my own.

Fortunately, the trail to Mount Baden-Powell is pretty popular and this calamity occurred on a Sunday, so the parking lot was full of day-hikers. I approached a young man eating a sandwich, explained my predicament, and asked for a ride. He not only dropped me off at a hotel, but gave me his number and said to call him at 6 the next morning and that we would go up there with ropes to retrieve the pack. I thanked him profusely as he dropped me off at a lodge. When the hotel owner learned of my difficulties, he offered to do my laundry for free and said I could wear some of his daughter's clothes in the meantime. We were about the same size, he figured.

I'm not quite sure whether this man was being genuinely nice or whether he just wanted to find out what I would look like in clothes about 3 sizes too small for me. I layered on the largest of the tiny clothes I could find and, arms across my chest, quickly dropped off my stinky laundry. Regardless of his motives, it was a boost to have clean clothes.

Now I turned my attention to getting organized for the morning. I looked for the piece of paper where I had written the name of the man who offered to help me. Incredibly, since his number was nearly all I had in my possession, I had lost it! I searched every pocket, every surface area I had touched since coming to town, asked the hotel proprietor about it, but it never turned up. More crying ensued. I decided to go to the local café to see if anyone there knew the guy. No one did, but the waitress told me if I didn't find him then she would make her boyfriend help me. She gave me her number. Next I went to the bar to see if anyone knew the man whose number I had lost. No one knew him there either, but another patron offered to help me instead. Leti turned out to be an EMT and a member of the search and rescue squad. She held certification in wilderness emergency care. In short, she was totally awesome.

The next morning, she drove me back out to the mountain. As we climbed, she pointed out many edible plants, explaining which were native and which had been introduced by settlers. She showed me two types of onions and a green vegetable called miner's lettuce. She also listened to my description of a plant with a two or three flower heads, with the top ones growing on a stalk emerging from the one below. This, she informed me, is chia. Her naturalist skills alone made her companionship invaluable!

I had picked up a couple of breakfast sandwiches to take with us. Even after summiting, we weren't hungry yet, so

I left them at the side of the trail near the spot where I had taken the wrong turn so that we could check out the scene unencumbered. (Okay, actually I was always hungry, but was trying to refrain from eating until Leti was ready for a meal.) From there we cast around until we found my pack, which leaned against a boulder several hundred feet down. She brought out the rope.

Leti sent me up to the ridge for a better view while she found a path most of the way down to my pack and tied the rope to a tree. (Does this sound to anyone like she might have just been trying to keep me out of her way?) She held to the rope as she descended the rest of the way to the pack. Once there, she tied the pack to the free end. Now she scampered back up to the tree and hauled the pack up the distance. Then she found another tree a bit higher up and repeated the process. Now that I had the idea, I came down to meet her and to help pull and push the pack up.

I had forgotten that I had left a compartment unzipped and we lost a few items, but nearly everything came through unscathed. I felt strangely reassured when Leti told me she was sure that I would have never been able to get up the ridge while wearing that pack. The scene I had been re-playing in my mind showed me needlessly leaving behind my possessions at the edge of a gentle slope. It was good to know that a fresh pair of eyes saw the situation the same way I had at the time I made my choice.

Once we had the pack most of the way up the ridge, I put it on my back and we found our way back to the trail. On the way down we stopped for a break. I broke out the sandwiches, one of which was half-eaten. I thought Leti must have grabbed a few bites while I was doing something else. So I grabbed the whole sandwich and offered her the rest of the one she had started. She politely declined. Only later did I learn that, in fact, a lovable hiker named Supergirl had seen the sandwiches there and taken the bites—not Leti. So my incredibly kind benefactor must have thought me pretty cheap to have offered her a half-eaten sandwich but she never said anything about it. In fact, she offered me her place to stay for the night.

Supergirl later told me he thought the sandwich was trail magic (something left intentionally for hikers). "Okay," I told him, "I can understand if you thought it was trail magic, but why on earth would you only take a few bites and leave the rest?" He never did give me a good answer for this thoroughly un-hikerly behavior.

Back at Leti's studio apartment, which she shared with her son, she offered me a shower. Just as I was stepping out and groping for my towel, a nosebleed began. At the same moment either Leti or her son knocked to let me know that they needed in there. I stuffed toilet paper up my nose and tried to put my clothes on while holding it in place. The blood soon soaked through, creating a bloody mess on the floor. "I'll be right out!" I claimed in an optimistic yet nasal tone. Every time I about had the bleeding stopped, I would bend to wipe the floor, and the change in position would start a fresh flow of blood. Another tentative knock. "Almost done!" I hollered. With a final wad of toilet paper freshly inserted, I finished dressing, wiped down the floor while holding more toilet paper to my face, and opened the door. As soon as I stood back up, the blood that had pooled at the tip of my nose came running back out. I headed for the paper towel. Poor Leti. No good deed goes unpunished. But she just laughed it off.

In spite of being reunited with my gear, I was steeped in doubts. How could I have gotten lost like that? When I saw where I had gone wrong, I couldn't believe it. The trail had been perfectly clear and there was no reason I should have taken a wrong turn there. Every hiker gets turned around at times, but I worried that maybe the next time wouldn't turn out so well for me. I questioned whether I just plain had the common sense a person ought to have if they want to hike the PCT. I called my friend Jessica to ask her opinion.

Jessica was the one person to whom I confided all my fears. She had received a slew of complaining, self-pitying letters from me. But she always told me to believe in myself, always said that although she would fully support whatever decision I made, she knew for sure that I was perfectly capable of completing this hike. When morning came, I decided to get back on that horse and hit the trail.

Leti had to go to work, so I bid her adieu and ambled to town to replace a few items that got lost in the rescue. There I ran into a couple out for their morning walk. They chatted with me and gave me their number, urging me to call when I needed a ride back to the trail. Hikers multiply. By the time I was ready to get picked up, I had met another hiker who also needed a ride.

Threshold was one of only two other hikers I met on the PCT who had a synthetic sleeping bag instead of a down-filled one. I carried synthetic because I decided not to upgrade to the more expensive down and also because I was worried it would get wet. Wet down makes a person colder, whereas a wet synthetic bag will allow a person to retain at least some body heat. Threshold used synthetic not because she was a cheap skate and worry wart like me, but because she is a vegan. Most vegans don't use any products that involve killing or maiming animals. Sadly, the down industry has much to answer for when it comes to treatment of animals.

The kind couple ferried us both back to the trail. Before dropping me off, they gave me some polyester running pants. I had lost my long pants in the mayhem on the ridge. Wrightwood lacked clothing stores (except for boutiques), so I was unable to replace them. Since the upcoming section of trail grew thick with poodle dog bush, I really needed long pants.

You are probably thinking that whatever poodle dog bush is, it is surely adorable. And actually it does bear quite a comely purplish blue flower. This usually rare plant grows almost exclusively in Southern California, and only after massive fire. As it happens, a massive fire ravaged the area a couple years earlier, leaving the trail now completely over-run with the bush. Unfortunately it causes serious rashes and painful blisters. The running pants were a godsend. I left Wrightwood light on self-confidence, but full of the milk of human kindness.

After being deposited by these kind trail angels, I found myself enjoying a rare shady stretch along a creek. Here I encountered two friendly hikers, Opus and Joe. They stopped for lunch while I carried on. Shortly thereafter, the trail entered a campground then veered out of the woods to resume its usual exposed, dusty tread.

An interesting crater-like depression sloped away on the left. My eye caught sight of two oncoming hikers. As they approached, we recognized each other. "Hello again," said Joe.

"Hi there," I replied. We nearly walked right past each other when I suddenly realized something wasn't right. "Um, one of us must be going the wrong way."

"Oh yeah," he responded while puzzlement spread over all three of our faces. "Well, it's not us."

I pulled out the map and compass. "I don't know. It looks like we are supposed to be going south briefly here and, well, I am going south right now."

Opus looked at the map. "I think this is just a short northward stretch that's not showing up on the map. We should turn south soon."

"But also, this depression is supposed to be on our left. And it is on my left."

"We have to be going the right way. We've been on the trail the whole time." Frustration waxed in Joe's voice.

Normally, I would have argued my case a little more strongly, but since I had just gotten lost on Baden-Powell, I uncharacteristically deferred to the judgment of others. "Okay, I'll turn around and walk with you guys a bit and see if we can figure it out."

We trod along for perhaps half a mile, with me meekly pointing out that we were still headed north instead of south. Finally I said that I really did not think this was right. We all stopped to allow Opus to pull out his smart phone to call up the GPS. It took some time to get a signal, but eventually, he determined that, in fact, he and Joe had been going the wrong way.

As we retraced our steps, we discussed how this could have happened. We all felt confident that we had stayed on the trail. Eventually, we realized that when they reached the campground, they hadn't noticed the spot where the trail veered away from the road. Serendipitously, the trail crossed the road a second time, just beyond the spot where I met them. There they rejoined the PCT, but headed the wrong direction, and that's how they met me.

I continued to leap-frog these guys for several days, and whenever we saw each other approaching, we liked to holler out, "Hey, aren't you going the wrong way?" Joe went home to visit his wife about a week later and I didn't see him so much after that, but I ended up hiking with Opus quite a bit over the next several hundred miles. I found him to be one of the most competent hikers and navigators around. After my experience on Baden-Powell, it made me feel a lot better to realize everyone gets turned around from time to time.

The following day started out gently, with a climb up into pine-forested elevations. At the top of a mountain, signs appeared announcing a detour. Not having any idea what lay in store, I started cheerfully enough down the gravel road which was the alternate route, but the next nine miles proved to be one of the least pleasant of my entire journey.

The road emerged from the forest and presented a scorching descent. Even with the use of my parasol, the heat was unlike anything I had yet encountered. The gravel soaked up the sun's rays, making my feet about as cool as if they were walking across hot coals. In the distance below I could see the Mill Creek Ranger Fire Station where water and shade awaited, but as the hours drew on, it never seemed to get any closer. The descent was tortuously gradual.

By the time I made it down to the sturdy little building, my face was beet-red. I collapsed in the shade of the porch. All the firefighters were away, and for a bit it was just me there. I found an outside spigot and guzzled water. Soon I was joined by equally wiped out Opus and Joe. Rather than starting up their stoves, they put their dehydrated food in a pan of water and simply set it out on the rocks. Twenty minutes later, they were eating a hot meal.

I pulled out my guidebook to read while waiting for some semblance of coolness to descend. Here I learned that I had just taken the Station Fire Detour, which steers hikers around the trail that had been damaged by a savage fire in 2009. According to the guidebook, the fire was started by a hiker who was burning his toilet paper. In the blaze that ensued, 251 square miles of forest were burned and two firefighters died, along with untold wildlife. Suddenly, I didn't feel like complaining quite so much about being too hot.

The firefighters now returned from a run mid-afternoon and asked if they could do anything to help us out. I wondered how it felt for them to have us hikers show up and hang around the station, when two of their colleagues had lost their lives as a result of a careless hiker. They were nothing but kind to us.

From here I carried on again to yet another detour. This one was optional and impromptu, for those who wished to

USING TOILET PAPER WHEN THERE'S NO TOILET

Though people are often too delicate to ask, many wonder what hikers do when nature calls.

When it comes to bowel movements, the responsible hiker digs a cat hole six inches deep and poops into it. There are then three main methods for dealing with the toilet paper. The first is to bury it, the second is to pack it out, the last is to forego the use of toilet paper altogether. The first option is the least reliable, as animals often dig it up and scatter it around like unfestive confetti. In heavy use areas, the ground can become quite disgusting.

I choose to pack it out, which isn't as gross as it might sound. It's no biggie to just tuck it into a baggy that is kept away from food and water. I was certainly always glad when I came upon a trash can where I could dispose of the baggie, but this option kept litter out of the backcountry.

The last option—that of not using toilet paper—sounds appalling, but most people throughout the world don't use toilet paper. There are a couple different systems to do this hygienically, though they involve more water than I liked to carry.

Regardless of which option is used, the best thing is to use some hand sanitizer afterward.

When it comes to taking a leak, I usually forego the toilet paper, instead grabbing some leaves or grass—though through much of the PCT the vegetation did not lend itself to my needs and I often had to air dry, which was rather unpleasant and not really very hygienic. Some women use toilet paper each time, but I didn't want to carry that much.

***

avoid massive quantities of poodle dog bush. It meant keeping to the exposed gravel road for several miles more, but I decided that such a route would be better than suffering severe blisters and rashes.

I hiked right up until sunset through the eerie burnt-out forest. When it came time to make camp, a strong wind kicked up. I looked up at all those dead trees, just waiting to fall on my tent. I selected a site surrounded by smaller trees which I hoped would not kill me if they fell on me. In spite of my safety concerns, that night I enjoyed one of the finest sunsets I've ever seen.

I tried to get up early the next day, though early rising has really never been my strong suit. I managed to get packed up and hiking around 5. By 7, I was lumbering up the last steep climb of the detour, with my parasol deployed. I heard foot-falls behind me. Along came Swami.

I had heard about Swami, a nice Australian man planning to hike more than 14,000 miles in 18 months. This sounded impossible to many, even in the community of long distance hikers. To be honest, many of us felt downright hostile to the idea. We would self-righteously assure each other that anyone who is cranking out 40 miles a day, day after day, was a miserable SOB who didn't understand how to enjoy the backpacking experience. My brief encounter with Swami changed my opinion completely.

Swami maintains a website called The Hiking Life, which I would heartily recommend to anyone at any level of back-packing. His love for the wilderness is infectious even when the medium is a lifeless computer screen. A complete novice would do well to read his suggestions, which are provid-ed with humility and candor. In a recent review of his site I learned plenty, even after having spent two decades as a backpacker and even as someone who does not aspire to an ultra-light, fast style.

Later, I would meet people who did high-mileage days and who really didn't seem to be enjoying themselves very much, but when I met Swami he was clearly doing exact-ly what he loved to do. His compact body must have just been built for churning out massive mileage, though he also employed his intellect to keep his pack light and navigation sound. He slowed down to chat with me for a bit, giving me news of various people behind me. Then he shifted back to his customary gait and with warm words of best wishes, he pushed ahead. I watched his tree-trunk-like legs carry him up the mountain as if it were nothing more than an anthill.

I later heard that Swami hadn't learned to identify poodle dog bush and ended up briefly in the emergency room with his body covered in blisters. His blog entry included this lament: "Lying in my motel bed I couldn't help but have an ironic chuckle in regards to my present situation. In some two decades of hiking around the globe, I have had close encounters with grizzlies, King Brown [cobras], rabid dogs, gun-toting Mexican bandits and roaring rapids. Who would have thought that I would finally be put out of action by an innocuous sounding plant by the name of 'Poodle Dog.'"

I now neared one of the great landmarks of Southern California—the Saufleys'. As with Ziggy and The Bear, I hadn't known anything about them until I heard other hikers counting down the days to their house. This incredible family opened their home every year to backpackers passing through the town of Agua Dulce (they have since retired from this practice). Hundreds of PCTers sent resupply packages there and still more took advantage of the offer of free laundry and shower. Other trail angels came to the Saufleys' to offer hikers rides to all kinds of places. To get there, I merely needed to cross Vasquez Rocks County Park, then get most of the way across town.

Several of us leap-frogged each other through this stretch. We all marveled at the wonderful boulder formations in the park, but were less impressed by the trail markings. I was headed up a small incline when two hikers named Steve and Alice met me coming back down.

"This isn't the PCT," they informed me, holding up their GPS. I knew this couple to be extremely reliable and capable hikers, but I really thought I was on the right path. They showed me their device, which I had no reason to doubt except that my reading of my map made me think I was headed in the right direction. Other hikers came along, all of us studying our various navigational tools. Steve and Alice, feeling certain they had found the right way, departed in the direction their GPS instructed. A couple other hikers did the same. Opus, Joe, and I stood together still undecided.

Joe pointed at the map, "Look, there is a sharp turn on the map, and we are at a sharp turn. We are going the right way!"

"Well, yes," I replied, "but there could be other sharp turns, this particular sharp turn doesn't have to be the one we see on the map." But Joe had already walked off. Opus and I looked at each other. "Even if this isn't the PCT, it will be easy enough to figure out how to get to Agua Dulce from here," I pointed out. Opus agreed, so off we went.

Although we shortly realized that, in fact, we were no longer on the PCT, we found ourselves walking along with a terrific view. From our vantage point, we could see the parasols of Steve and Alice bobbing along the correct route, so at least we had our bearings. We kept to our trail. Opus cleverly deduced that since this was a small county park, all trails were likely to lead back to the main parking lot at some point, and we could pick up the PCT there. However, I could see town to the east, and when the trail veered sharply to the west (toward the parking lot), I decided I would just cut cross country to where the trail joined the road while they stuck to their plan.

I got slightly turned around trying to find a way out of a pasture, but soon made my way to the blistering hot sidewalks of Agua Dulce. I felt kind of sheepish for leaving my friends behind, but needn't have worried. A truck pulled over and Joe hollered from the bed, "Hey want a ride?" He extended his hand to haul me into the back of the pickup.

"Where's Opus?"

"The sun must be getting to him. He said he'd rather walk," Joe replied.

Everyone hikes the trail in their own way. Some people want to hike every step of the PCT. Others don't feel the need to stay on the trail itself, but do insist on at least having continuous footsteps from one border to the other. Then there are people like me. I didn't set out feeling all that attached to completing the trail in any fashion. I frankly had assumed I would have broken an ankle by now, and felt pleasantly surprised to have made it this far at all. In general my goal was not so much to make it from one border to the other, but more to learn new things and enjoy myself. I felt that walking on roads rarely contributed to either of these goals, and so I never objected to skipping road sections if I could. I couldn't help but admire Opus for walking every step, but I was relieved not to have such high standards for myself.

The driver dropped us off right at the Saufleys', where we were met by a woman volunteering to help the family get through the busy season. Sweet Cindy greeted us with big hugs. Really big hugs. I was afraid for a moment that she was going to wrap her legs around me. She gazed into my eyes. "Welcome," she spoke solemnly and lovingly.

Oh that's right, I thought, I'm in California.

Sweet Cindy showed me around, explaining the ingeniously efficient systems the Saufleys had developed to take care of the needs of their grimy guests. In short order, I had managed to get a shower, do laundry and catch a ride to an outdoor gear store to replace the jogging pants with some more light-weight attire.

Upon my return, the crowd of hikers began to fray my nerves and I made a plan to get back to the trail first thing in the morning. When Sweet Cindy heard the news, she informed me that since she wouldn't be up that early, she would have to give me all my hugs that night. I panicked.

I would be tarred and feathered sooner than endure more of those inappropriately intense hugs. How could I prevent them without being rude to such a nice person?

"Well, actually, I'm from the Midwest," I explained, "and we don't really hug."

She countered that plenty of Midwesterners had given her hugs.

"Yes, but I'm from northern Wisconsin. It takes us years to move from a handshake to a hug."

Still, she persisted by explaining the virtues of hugs, and I persisted in describing myself as an ever more neurotic person who would be damaged by further hugging. At last, she conceded that if I didn't want a hug then no hugs would be forthcoming.

Not five minutes later, I heard someone exclaim, "Hey, NightinGail!" I turned to see a bearded man opening his arms for a hug. Through the fog of my prosopagnosia I made what turned out to be a correct guess that this was Doc, a hiker I hadn't seen for hundreds of miles. He and his partner Blue Jay were great company and I was so happy to see them that I would have certainly accepted his friendly embrace if not for the fact that I had just declared myself allergic to any and all hugs.

"Uh, hi," I said awkwardly while Sweet Cindy looked on. I kept my arms firmly at my sides while I stiffly inquired, "How are you?"

I wouldn't see Doc again for 200 miles to explain why I hadn't reciprocated his enthusiasm.

Incredibly, the last of a trio of famous trail angels in Southern California are situated only a day's walk from the Saufleys'. I planned to skip the home of the Andersons, especially since the latter had a reputation as a good place to party, and the partying at the Saufleys' had been more than enough for me. But 24 blistering miles later, I reconsidered.

Just where the trail intersected the highway that led to the Andersons', a car pulled up. "Get in!" hollered the young woman at the wheel. I didn't need to be told twice, and neither did Supergirl who happened to be hiking with me just then. We piled inside, and cold beverages were immediately placed in our hands. A few minutes later we pulled into a yard where a raucous crowd milled about. When we stepped from the car, everyone applauded as if we had just given birth to Einstein.

"Grab a shirt," someone instructed, pointing to a rack. I looked around and noticed everyone was decked out in bowling shirts. Except for the hostess, who sported an obscene apron and a halo headband.

I scanned the rack and immediately found the shirt for me. Unbeknownst to the crowd here, this was not actually a bowling shirt. With flames racing up blue rayon fabric, this style had been quite fashionable in the inner cities some years hence. I knew I would look incredibly absurd in it, so that's the one I chose.

"What's your name?" asked a woman volunteering for the week.

"NightinGail," I replied, but when I saw her expression I realized this no longer worked. "I need something more awesome to match this shirt, don't I?"

"Uh, yeah," she replied. "Like, NIGHTRIDER!"

Thus it was that certain hikers who met me that night continued to call me Nightrider for a few hundred miles.

The Andersons' turned out to be one of my favorite non-wilderness places on the entire trail. I love quirky, irreverent people. Mrs. Anderson, in particular, captured my heart with her randomly strict rules and rituals, her kindheartedness, and her storytelling.

Here, too, I first met the botanist thru-hiker Peru. I had heard of her for some time and often imagined how wonderful it would be to have her expertise as I traipsed through such unfamiliar terrain. "Oh, you're the botanist, right? Can I ask you a few questions?" I gushed.

She fixed me with a withering look and slowly articulated, "Now is not the time to play 'ask-a-botanist.'"

Ouch. Hundreds of miles later we would meet again and she would explain that she hadn't meant to be rude. Rather, she had been in her cups and was struggling to succinctly explain that she was not in the best condition for scientific conversation.

In the morning I accidentally broke one of the Andersons' rules by taking coffee from the pot intended for their own personal consumption. Mr. Anderson gruffly asked what I thought I was doing, but when I apologized profusely, he winked and said, "It'll be our secret. You can even have your second cup from this pot—it's way better than what we give everyone else."

I apparently wasn't the only hiker who enjoyed the place. I met some who had been there for nearly a week! Much as I had a great time, I still felt eager to set off the following afternoon. With all the rest under my belt, I started to believe that I might actually make it as far as the Sierra Nevada mountain range, now only a little more than 200 miles away.

For some time, I had been putting in roughly 20-mile days, occasionally going as few as 17 or as many as 24 miles in a day. I had plateaued in that mileage range and was curious what it would be like to really push myself. Thus it was that a few days later I found myself navigating my way through endless canyons as darkness fell, putting in a 32-mile day. I was headed for a resupply point known as Hikertown.

Once I entered a certain parcel of private property, it was all or nothing because the owners did not permit camping. One would think that if a property holder were hostile to accepting hikers on their land, then they would want us to get off their territory as quickly and with as little disruption to the terrain as possible. I would be sympathetic to such a desire. But they insisted instead on a route that hugs the boundary of the ranch in seven pointless miles, rather than routing us on a dirt road which would have us through the parcel in no time. Signs warn hikers that they might wander into a stray bullet by target shooters if they step off trail.

When I finally made it in and out of every last everlasting canyon on the ranch, I had to cross a highway, then walk along that highway for a stretch to reach Hikertown. In the darkness, I lost the trail. Eventually I had to leap a fence and scuttle down a steep embankment to reach the road. By this time, my feet cramped like crazy and hunger pangs attacked my innards. The wind whipped and howled all around me, forcing me to strain forward.

Upon closing the distance to Hikertown, the place stood quiet and almost completely dark. I quietly unlatched the gate to slip inside. I closed the gate again behind me and stepped forward toward a small light in a window. That's when the dogs rushed me.

I bolted back to the gate. In record time I opened it, flew through, and slammed it behind me. My heart beat wildly as the dogs jumped and writhed on the other side of the welded wire.

A man emerged from one of the buildings and told me it was perfectly safe to come in. Hesitantly, I re-entered the compound. The dogs obeyed his command to let me alone. For $10, he showed me to a strange little building labeled "Doctor." Inside, a foldout mattress beckoned. I asked the man where I could go in the morning to pick up my resupply boxes. He kindly offered to let me get them right then. He opened another little building labeled "Post Office." Inside, parcels and letters lay scattered across the floor. Together, we found my resupply box and, better still, a box of cookies from my mom and another from my aunt.

I returned to the Doctor's office and tore into the cookies. Exhaustion made proper dinner preparation impossible, so I ate one cookie after another. Only as I was wiping the crumbs from my chin did I realize I had eaten them so quickly that I didn't even know what kind they were. Peanut butter? Chocolate chip? And why was I in a building labeled "Doctor?" I had no idea about any of it. Ignoring the silverfish running around the mattress, I lay down. As soon as the throbbing in my feet ebbed, I fell asleep even as the wind played drumsticks with everything not battened down.

The next morning, the intensity of the howling wind only increased. I woke with the sun and, looking out the window, noticed a hiker leaving out the front gate. I stretched, rose, and began investigating how I could obtain a shower and do laundry. I fought my way across the blustery courtyard toward a hiker lounge. I passed more little buildings labeled with names like "Sheriff" and "Hotel."

When I reached the hiker lounge, I tugged and fought against the wind to open the door, then fought even harder to close it again. A few hikers were already milling about inside. Nimblefoot asked me if I had seen his hiking poles, but I hadn't. As the morning went along, he asked more people this same question, but with increasing concern. After a couple hours of having looked everywhere and asked everyone, he concluded that the poles must have been stolen.

This sounded absurd to me. In all my years of backpacking, I had never known anyone to lose any of their gear to theft. First of all, most backpackers, like most people everywhere, are too honest to steal. Secondly, if a backpacker weren't honest, he or she would still be disinclined to carry one ounce more and thus would curb thieving ambitions. Surely someone had simply moved Nimblefoot's poles and they would turn up.

By noon, however, everyone agreed the poles were nowhere to be seen. Someone asked which hikers had left Hikertown since the last time Nimblefoot had seen them. The only hiker he knew for sure who had left was Sunny. "He could have taken them," Nimblefoot insisted. "He didn't have poles of his own, so he wouldn't have had to get rid of anything to take them."

At this I perked up. "Sunny didn't have hiking poles?" If he was the only hiker who had left, then he had to have been the hiker I saw leaving the compound that morning. I wasn't positive, but I thought I had seen that hiker using trekking poles.

That sealed it. The proprietor of Hikertown got in his truck and took off after Sunny. This stretch of the trail uncharacteristically follows roads for about 20 miles, and he came upon Sunny—with Nimblefoot's poles—at about mile 16.

When the proprietor returned, he gave Nimblefoot his poles, but was too upset to tell us very much about what had happened. We gathered that he had lost his dog, who always rode along in the truck. When he stopped to confront Sunny, the dog jumped out. In spite of searching and calling for some time, the dog never came back. I very much hope the pooch eventually made her way home across that desolate landscape. I hate to think about her wandering alone in that waterless land.

When we hikers were left to ourselves again, a number of stories emerged about Sunny. He had stolen one person's sunglasses, taken another person's pants. He had stiffed trail angels who mailed packages for him, and so on. Perhaps these stories weren't true. Even if they were, I suppose one rotten apple in 20 years of backpacking isn't such a bad average, but I found the whole incident quite upsetting.

I hung out at Hikertown until late afternoon, resting up for the next segment of trail that would take me across the floor of the Mojave Desert. Like most hikers, I planned to do at least the first 17 miles as a night hike to avoid the brutal heat. I set out sometime after 4 p.m. The wind knocked me around like a pinball until about 8.

EVERY STITCH OF CLOTHING I PACKED

I started the trail with some items I planned on swapping out as the opportunity arose. In particular, I wanted to lose anything cotton. I knew that stores and hotels and other places that see a lot of hikers often have a box where people can leave gear and food that they no longer want. I hoped to pick up some clothes this way. I did, and also ended up purchasing some new items.

What I Started With	What I Ended With
4 pairs of socks (wearing 2 pairs at a time)	2 pairs of socks (wearing one pair at a time)
Khaki pants	Polyester hiking pants
2 cotton t-shirts	1 polyester short-sleeved shirt
1 fleece jacket	1 down jacket
1 pair of long johns	Same pair of long johns
1 shade hat	Same shade hat (badly misshapen by a dryer incident in Northern California)
3 pairs of underwear, plus five extra crotches attached by Velcro so that I could have a fresh bit of cloth at the pertinent parts	5 pairs of underwear, plus two inserts
Nylon shorts	No separate shorts (the legs of my hiking pants zipped off)
1 long-sleeved button-up shirt and 1 long-sleeved fleece shirt	2 long-sleeved polyester shirts
1 bra	Same bra (largely useless at this point)
1 pair of light-weight gloves	2 pairs of light-weight gloves

1 pair of mittens	Same pair of mittens (but I shipped them home between Idyllwild and mid-Washington)
1 warm hat	Same warm hat + 1 balaclava
1 scarf	Same scarf
1 rain jacket	Same rain jacket
1 pair of rain pants	Same rain pants

***

Early on, I fell in with a hiker named Wrong Way. Like Swami, he racked up thousands of miles over the course of high-mileage days. In fact, he had already met Swami on three different trails, most recently coming up Mount Baden-Powell on the PCT.

I appreciated Wrong Way. As an active member of his Ironworkers local union, he provided a kind of conversation I missed tremendously. We shared many of the same views on labor and politics and we each came from a working class background. He had even helped to build a bridge not far from my Wisconsin home! For these reasons, and also because I wanted to see if I could keep up with such a strong hiker, I resolved to keep pace with him as far as I could. This resulted in me pushing out the entire 17 miles to Cottonwood Creek Bridge without any break. I shouldn't complain, for him it was the end of a 40-mile day.

The sky lacked any moon to help us find our way, and by the end we started to become concerned that we had taken a wrong turn—Wrong Way pointed out that he had been given his trailname for a reason. Just as our sore feet and our uncertainty had us teetering on the brink of irritability, we found camp around 11 p.m. Fortunately, the piped water source there was functioning—which I later learned only happened when the planets aligned just so. We found a note alerting us to the presence of bobcat kittens playing under the bridge at dawn and dusk. I was too exhausted to contemplate either the potential danger or the certain cuteness that this must have entailed.

I descended toward the dry creek-bed to find a place to pitch my tent. With such violent wind, I should have foregone the tent, but I always worried about snakes crawling into my sleeping bag if I roughed it. I did leave part of the shelter unattached from the frame to keep it from catching the wind quite so much. Other hikers piled into the site around 1:30 in the morning. None of us slept much in that gale.

I broke camp shortly after Wrong Way, but his strong pace carried him much farther much faster than my own shambling gait. In the months ahead I occasionally learned of his whereabouts when I read a trail register he had signed. But for now I left behind the still-sleeping bodies of the late-arrivers in order to tackle the rest of the trek through the Mojave on my own.

Ever since I had set off from the Mexican border, I had been dreading this part of the hike. For most hikers, this is the hottest stretch of the trail, and it is largely waterless. It was now May 23, and even at higher elevations, the temperature was usually virtually unbearable by 7 in the morning. I shuddered to imagine what it would be like down here right on the floor of the Mojave. I certainly was relieved to have completed the first 17 miles of this stretch in the evening, but many miles still remained.

Instead of the gruelingly hot stretch I anticipated, this proved to be one of the coldest days on my entire hike. Deserts are bizarre that way. The pervasive wind turned bitter and grew ever stronger. By the time I reached Tylerhorse Creek seven miles later, I had accoutered myself with nearly every stitch of clothing I packed and I was wiped out from fighting the gusts. I hoped to find some shelter

at this site, but no large boulders or trees presented themselves. I refilled my water and shiveringly shoved food in
my mouth.

As I stood up to leave, another hiker named Castle came
down the canyon. She had arrived to Cottonwood Creek in
the wee hours of the morning and hence had risen much later
than me. Although only in her mid-20s, she already had a de-
cade of experience as a backpacker. She hiked as powerfully
as her name implied, and one always got the sense that, so
long as she had her backpack, she was doing what she loved.
Thus, her long face took me aback. The lack of sleep combined with the atrocious conditions had taken its toll even on
my sturdy friend. I would have liked to have stayed to keep
her company while she ate lunch and to try to lift her spirits,
but I had to get moving to warm up. Plus, I still had 17 miles
to go before reaching the road where I hoped to catch a ride
into town that night.

The temperature warmed somewhat as the day progressed, allowing me to shift the focus of my misery from
the weather to my blistered feet. I put in a few relatively enjoyable miles before the weather changed again. I had only
thought the wind blew powerfully before. In the final eight
miles, the effort to simply remain on my feet commanded
all of my attention. Again and again, gusts nearly blew me
right off the steep mountainside. I strained with every step to
make progress against the invisible wall of its force. Periodically, just as I would lean hard into the gale, the wind would
stop for just an instant and I would pitch forward, nearly
falling now from the lack of nature's force.

The trail traversed exposed ridges, leaving me no shelter
for even a moment. Up to this point, I had often considered
dropping off the trail for various reasons, but this was the first
time that I questioned whether I possessed the sheer physical strength necessary to complete the hike. I had to summon
every last reserve of energy to push my way through these

final miles of the day. By the end, I no longer had enough power in my legs to always keep my balance, and a number of times the wind pushed me all the way to the ground. I clawed at juniper bushes and clambered against the invisible force to regain the trail.

I finally caught a glimpse of road a couple of miles away. The sight buoyed me somewhat, but I still didn't feel totally confident in the odds that I would make it there rather than plummet to my death. At times like this, I wished I had a hiking companion. Not that another person would have prevented me from falling, but at least they could have witnessed the event and told my loved ones some noble lie about how I died painlessly.

In the midst of this despair, two hikers overtook me. Salty Snacks and Cheetah came bounding down the mountain. "Isn't this amazing?" Cheetah exclaimed. She threw her bandana up into the air and then raced the wind down the mountain to snatch it again.

"It is amazing," I said with a phony smile. I wanted it to be amazing instead of terrifying and exhausting. I thought if I were a better backpacker, I would be having the time of my life right now.

"See you at the road!" they called as they hurried on their way.

I watched their energetic descent toward the pavement and I tried to hold onto some of Cheetah's enthusiasm. When the wind knocked me over for the umpteenth time and I found myself clinging to a fortuitously placed shrub to hoist myself upright again, the enthusiasm ebbed.

At long last, I made my way far enough down the mountain that I could tell I would make it all the way, but my mood had gone sour again. A day-hiker approached from the opposite direction. Searching for some comfort, I asked, "Is it always this windy here?"

The twerp looked at me like I were some kind of idiot. He pointed at the wind turbines dotting the entire landscape. "I'm not from here, but I would guess it is always windy."

Between Cheetah's joy and this man's disdain, I felt I must be a truly sorry excuse of a backpacker to be so miserable right then. Upon reaching the foot of the mountain, I again met Cheetah and Salty. The latter was now openly crabby and told me that although he had tried to match Cheetah's mood, the simple truth was that today's hike had been downright horrible. Salty is the kind of hiker who is capable of 40-mile days in all kinds of weather. I continued to see him off and on all the way through Oregon, but this was the only time I can ever remember him complaining about conditions. Perhaps I wasn't such a pathetic hiker after all.

I had thought I would reach the road by late afternoon, but it was now 7:45 p.m. I knew I had to stick my thumb out quick if I wanted to catch a ride. Mojave lay about 12 miles to the east, Tehachapi about eight miles to the west. I figured I would take the first ride that came along in either direction. Soon enough, a truck pulled over heading west. I threw my pack in the back and climbed inside. The kind driver took note of my bedraggled appearance and assured me that, in fact, it was not always this windy here at all. Yes, it was a good site for wind turbines, but today's gusts were quite unusual. Those words gave me back my sense of perspective and possibly prevented me from quitting the hike then and there.

Later I would find out that the day's sustained winds of 95 mph had blown the roof off a hotel, snapped telephone poles, and made national news. At the time, all I knew was that every hiker I met in town looked just as shell-shocked as I did. I dined with Opus and a hiker named Stride that evening. We agreed that nobody except the hikers who came through that day of wind could understand the experience.

To recap the last three days: First I did a 32-mile day. Then I did a mere 17 miles, but at a 3.5 mph pace and with no breaks. I got virtually no sleep before undertaking the final 24 windswept miles into town. I was battered, blistered, exhausted. I badly wanted to take a zero-mileage day and rest in town, but that wasn't in the budget. On a whim, I called a local magazine and asked if they would be interested in running a story about the PCT. They were thrilled with the idea and willing to pay for it.

I rushed downstairs to the hotel computer and began pounding out my experiences thus far. In the morning I did a little rewriting and proofreading before sending it off. The editor wrote back to let me know the story was accepted and that they would cut me a check. That covered the extra night in town.

When I stopped by their office to pick up my payment, the office manager offered to give me a ride back to the trail. As we neared the trailhead, I half-jokingly said, "I guess this means I have to hike now." Even with the full day of rest behind me, I couldn't walk quite normally.

The woman at the wheel informed me that if another day of rest was what I needed, then I should stay at her place. By now I was getting used to being a mooch, so I readily accepted her offer. The extra day did me a world of good physically and mentally. Best of all, by the time she dropped me off the next day, she and I had become fast friends.

In spite of the renewed resilience I gained from this reprieve, the wind almost defeated me yet again. The first few miles back on the trail brought gusts nearly as strong as before. Again and again, it knocked me off trail, and this time the terrain fell away even more steeply than before. The wind also blew colder. Although I donned my gloves, I completely lost sensation in my fingers. When I came across a stunted grove of shrubs, I ducked into it for some shelter.

Out of the howling wind, I dug numbly through my pack to find spare socks. With the help of my teeth, I pulled the socks over my gloves. Then I tucked each hand into an armpit. While I waited for feeling to return, I took stock of my options.

Other hikers had told me that the next hundred miles to Walker Pass were always very windy. I felt unsure how to evaluate the situation. If this were the level of gusts that I could expect for the next few days, I frankly wasn't sure I would make it to Walker Pass in one piece. On the other hand, if I were just getting the worst of it now and the gales moderated a few miles on, then I could do it. My choices were to turn back to Tehachapi and from there either leave the trail altogether or skip ahead past Walker Pass, or to keep going and see what happened. The problem with the second option was that there were not many good places to get off the trail before Walker Pass if I changed my mind. The problem with the first option—besides the fact that it would sort of make me a coward—was that it would mean that I would have to go back through what had already been a treacherous traverse.

At this point, in spite of the wind and any other hardship, I was becoming attached to the hiking lifestyle. I had to at least try to continue.

When my hands thawed sufficiently, I pulled out my map. I saw I was about to cross a high ridge, and it seemed to me that the wind might abate on the other side of it. I shouldered my pack and pressed on. The wind continued to buffet me about for the remaining few hundred feet that I had yet to climb. Then, the instant I crossed the ridge, it fell completely silent. Within minutes the gloves came off and my high spirits returned. The microclimates of mountainous terrain never cease to fascinate me.

I camped with several other hikers that night near a spring. One of them had found a sock on the trail. She proffered it to every person she saw to find out if it was theirs. I commented that she was a better person than me, because that same day I had found a pair of sunglasses but I had left them on the trail rather than carry the added weight in what I expected would be a vain search for the owner.

The other hikers chastised me. "Ohhh … that's not good. You've acquired some bad gear karma." Of course we all laughed it off as the joke that it was. But I'll be darned if the next day I didn't ruin my own sunglasses. I can't explain it. I set the sunglasses in my pocket for a brief moment, as I had many times before. When I pulled them out again, they were utterly mangled. Not just broken, but mangled. Shortly afterward, the pin felt out of my watchband and I nearly lost my timepiece. By the end of the day I had also lost my pocket knife when it fell out of my pocket. From that day forward, I always tried to find the owners of lost gear.

Less than a week lay between me and the end of desert hiking. On the morning of the third day I was down to one liter of water and needed to push ahead to a place where some trail angels reportedly had left a cache near a road. I roused myself at 4 to catch that ever-shrinking window of cool morning air. I arrived at the road in the full heat of the sun at 7 a.m. It's difficult to describe the relief I felt to find that the cache was full. Without it, I would not have had a lot of cheerful options. I suppose I would have found the best shade I could and waited for nightfall to hike on again to water, but I would have been pretty dehydrated by then.

From the cache, I took the minimum amount of water I needed to last me the distance to the next spring. As I was getting ready to hoist the pack and move on again, another hiker approached. Even with my prosopagnosia I knew I had never met him before because this man had a totally unique style.

Most hikers considered my 40-pound pack absurdly heavy and bulky, but Duane's huge backpack must have weighed in around 55 pounds. Even more astonishingly, he also wore a daypack! This he strapped backwards so that it was across his chest.

"Well, I sure am glad to see this water!" He called out in a thick southern drawl. He began rummaging around in his pack, removing various empty bottles. "It sure is a hot morning and it looks like it's going to be another hot day. This water is going to taste real good. I don't like to get low on water. Or food either. People always ask me about my two packs. I just like to carry enough food and water to last me awhile. I started the hike with another guy that I met on the Appalachian Trail but he only wanted to do 30-mile days and I like to just go and go. After a while we had to split up. My name's Duane by the way."

On and on he went. Nothing about Duane was halfway. I later learned that other hikers referred to him as "Insane Duane" because of his eccentricities, but I never met a person who meant it in anything but an affectionate way. How could we help but admire this man whose body seemed designed to fly up and down mountains with a heavy load? And although I was bowled over by the volume of conversation, how could I find his cheery demeanor and earnest friendliness anything but pleasing?

"I don't carry no maps," he continued, "so I like to have extra food in case I get lost."

The number of hikers who forego maps amazes me. In particular, many of the high-mileage hikers didn't seem to bother with them. I always assumed that it was part of the ultra-light mentality, but here was a man who clearly didn't mind carrying a few extra ounces.

"No ma'am, I don't carry no maps. And yes I do get lost. One time I went 18 miles in the wrong direction, but I carry

20 days' worth of food, so it don't matter! I don't worry, I just know God will get me there."

I left him there in order to begin the ascent ahead. On the way up I met a day-hiker who gave me an energy bar, saying that he figured I needed it more than he did. By this time I was quite unashamed to take advantage of all opportunities to increase my caloric intake so I thanked him and wolfed it down. While still on the lower switchbacks, I registered rapid footsteps behind me. They belonged to energetic Duane, who practically skipped up the steep incline.

"That sure was a nice man down there. He gave me an apple. These day-hikers are so kind sometimes, aren't they? One time this other fella I met... ." And so on.

When he had walked along with me for a little while longer, he suddenly wished me all kinds of luck and bounced forward again, quick and nimble as a mountain goat. That was the last I ever saw of Duane.

That evening I stumbled into Walker Pass campground. Here, friends of a fellow hiker named Paws had come down from Oregon to keep him company for a bit. They decided to bestow some beer and chocolate on any other hikers that strolled into camp that night. Since they had a car, I asked them if they happened to have a cheap pair of sunglasses in the vehicle that I could buy off them. No they didn't, but Paws piped up to say that he had found a pair just the other day. He was just waiting for a chance to call the owner, named Clay, who had put his name and phone number in the case.

I was pretty desperate for some sunglasses, especially since I would shortly be starting the Sierra Nevadas, where the thinner air and snow make the sun that much more painful and destructive. So I proposed that I could take Clay's sunglasses just for the time being and that I would call him at the first opportunity to find out where to send them. I figured that whenever I reached a place where I could ship sunglasses I would also be in a town where I could find some cheap ones for sale. I didn't like taking someone else's gear, what with my karma already in such a problematic state, but I couldn't see how I was doing anything wrong.

Clay, by the way, had good taste in sunglasses. From the first moment I donned them, I suddenly understood why people pay a lot of money for good ones. I dreaded the moment I would surely somehow destroy this admirable pair.

Whatever worries I had about eyewear paled in comparison to the troubles of another camper at Walker Pass that night. Sampson had encountered the dreaded poodle dog bush. The rash became so infected that he ended up in the emergency room at a nearby hospital earlier that day. Even now, one of his hands was so puffy it looked like a grotesque balloon and was completely useless to him. This limitation in no way prevented him from opening chocolate bars and beers. He was, after all, a true hiker.

Now only two days of hiking stood between me and the beginning of the Sierras. If I had any intention of lingering, it would have been put to rest by the blistering heat served up in that final stretch. I hustled as much as I could with a blister on my heel so deep and raw that I had to force myself literally every step of the way. I no longer had a true gait, but rather something more like a sliding hop. My needle had long since become too dull to be of much use in popping blisters like this, but I nonetheless forced the blunt instrument into the skin again and again trying to reduce the swelling. With all the sweating I was doing, no covering would stay over the blister, though I applied duct tape to it a few times a day. The one positive thing I can say about this massive wound was that the pain was so intense that it dwarfed the pain from all my lesser blisters.

I stopped for lunch at Joshua Spring, where signs warned that the water was contaminated with uranium. Somewhere

FOOT CARE

All hikers agree that foot care is of utmost importance. Here are some of the things I have learned.

- Buy the best insoles you can and make sure they are the right ones for your feet. I have flat feet and need a lot of arch support, for example.
- Avoid waterproof linings in your boots or shoes.
- Remove shoes and socks at every break. Set them in the sun to dry out.
- Stretch and exercise your foot muscles at night and at breaks.
- Elevate feet at breaks, if possible.
- Stop hiking the moment you feel a blister coming. Remove shoes and socks and get it covered. This is harder than it sounds, since almost nothing adheres for very long to sweaty skin. Moleskin is useless. Climbing tape works passably well if you can get it and sometimes I found a hiker with some very expensive brand of tape that worked well. I typically used duct tape. Deciding whether to lance a blister before covering it is something that comes with experience. Sometimes it's best to let them be, other times lancing is essential.

***

I seemed to remember that they give iodine tablets to people that have radiation poisoning. This vague and possibly inaccurate bit of info was enough to assuage my worries, since I happened to carry iodine as a back-up water purifier. I used the tablets and drank it down.

After lunch I planned to march on up the 1,000-foot ascent ahead, but the heat crippled me. When I came across a shade tree—that rarest of commodities in Southern California—I decided not to let the opportunity pass. I set myself in the deepest part of its shade and fell sound asleep. Twice,

I was woken by what I thought were the penetrating rays of the shifting sun beating down on me. However, when I opened my eyes each time I found that I still lay safely in the shade; the ambient air had become so hot that it felt like direct sunlight.

I finally pushed myself on again around 3 p.m. and climbed up and then down to the pitiful Spanish Needle Creek, which I nonetheless took water from before making one last ascent to reach a high beautiful campsite among Joshua trees just as darkness fell.

The following day—the last full day in Southern California—I came through a large burned-out area that would have been rather joyless if not for the company of Moonshine and Supergirl, who found me lollygagging on a long break and spurred me on. They passed me after a while, but their companionship had cheered me through the worst part of the afternoon. That night I camped only four miles from Kennedy Meadows and the start of the Sierras.

Southern California had proved a challenge unlike any I've faced in the backcountry. From the heat to the blisters, from the overabundance of humans to the lack of greenery, these 700 miles forced me to call upon reserves of strength I hadn't known I possessed. And they forced me to realize how dependent I was on the encouragement of friends as well as the kindness of strangers. For all this, I will always be grateful. And in spite of the difficulties, even if I had not taken one more step on the PCT, I would have already seen a lifetime's worth of stunning flowers, gorgeous vistas, phenomenal sunsets, and eerie beauty.

Yet what nature had in store next surpassed all I had witnessed thus far.

At this stage in Southern California, my blisters would get worse before they got better.

Photo by Gail Francis.

Train glides down the dusty trail in one of the 26 wedding dresses he wore on the hike.

Photo by Knut Skarsem.

The Summer Solstice was the coldest night of the hike! Here I am bundled up and inside my sleeping bag.

Photo by Knut Skarsem.

I found a peaceful spot to rest with Collector (L) and Memphis (R) near Ebbetts Pass.

Photo by Knut Skarsem.

Many hikers found the forests of Northern California tedious and preferred the high crestlines, but I loved the magical quality of trees like this one in the Desolation Wilderness.

Photo by Knut Skarsem.

Knut was the later riser of the two of us at this campsite on Hat Creek Rim.

Photo by Gail Francis.

Hikers often made ephemeral signs to let each other know when a certain milestone had been achieved.

Photo by Gail Francis.

The landowner along this stretch of trail in Oregon seemed very concerned that PCT hikers would trespass. Another sign helpfully informed us that "If you can read this, you are in range."

Photo by Knut Skarsem.

Crater Lake alone would have been worth the hike!

Photo by Knut Skarsem.

When Gourmet was briefly reunited with his saxophone, we all benefited from the music he made.

Photo by Knut Skarsem.

In the Three Sisters Wilderness, the day was unusually hot, and the Obsidian Falls brought incredible joy and relief.

Photo by Knut Skarsem.

The trail was often a bit narrow and the drop-offs a bit steep, as in the case of the Eagle Creek detour we took.

Photo by Knut Skarsem.

On my way to Tunnel Falls (look closely to see me on the trail to the right of the falls).

Photo by Knut Skarsem.

Even after all my hard work, Jessica LaBumbard still beat me at arm wrestling.

Photo by Knut Skarsem.

The Goat Rocks Wilderness—if I had to choose a single most gorgeous day of the hike, it might have been the stretch along this knife-edge.

Photo by Gail Francis.

Other hikers made fun of me for being a little unsteady on my feet sometimes when needing to cross rivers via fallen logs. I preferred crawling to striding whenever possible.

Photo by Knut Skarsem.

This creek crossing was harder than it looked, in part because it was on a steep descent, and in part because I had just thrown out my back.

Photo by Knut Skarsem.

In order to preserve a little bit of hygiene, I tried to avoid eating anything with my filthy hands. Hence the spoon in this bag of almonds at Cutthroat Pass in Washington.

The monument at the border with Canada!

Photo by Knut Skarsem.

The last word should always go to good friends. Many thanks to Gabriela and Joaquin Pastor for driving up from Portland to pick us up at Manning Provincial Park. A wonderful end to a wonderful journey.

CENTRAL CALIFORNIA

On June 1, after six weeks in the deserts of Southern California, I reached Kennedy Meadows—the southern portal to the majestic High Sierras of central California. (Not to be confused with another Kennedy Meadows near the northern end of the range.) Here a trail angel named Tom runs a large camp that, along with a nearby store, serves as the staging area for hikers preparing for this new phase of the hike.

Nearly everyone needs to change their gear at least a little bit here, and in most years solo hikers partner up at this point before ascending into the high snowy passes. All through the first 700 miles, we hikers continually discussed the High Sierras. We shared updates on conditions of the passes and the fords. We compared intentions with regard to gear. We told stories of previous experiences in the majestic range. We focused so much on the Sierras, I scarcely knew what came after.

This, however, was the golden year of the PCT. Whereas the previous year brought record snowfall to the High Sierras, this year was almost devoid of snow. When planning the trip, I had worried a lot about the high passes. I didn't have much experience on snow or ice and I couldn't decide the best way to outfit myself. Nearly everyone recommends carrying an ice axe for this stretch, but I had never used one and wasn't sure the best type to buy. As the winter wore on with still no major snowfall being reported in the mountains, I sat on my money and took a wait and see approach.

By the time I arrived in Kennedy Meadows on June 1, it was perfectly obvious that snow would only be an obstacle on a few of the high passes, if then. The majority of hikers forewent their ice axes and almost none brought crampons. Even so, my inexperience led me to feel apprehensive about doing this stretch alone.

Apart from concern about safety, my hope of latching onto another hiker or two had an emotional component. I had heard much about how people group together at Kennedy Meadows and I remembered how I was always the last to be picked for kickball as a kid. I am blessed with the world's finest friendships, but I've never been a big winner in general popularity contests. Although nearly all the other hikers were unfailingly warm and helpful to me, I hadn't formed any particular bonds with anyone since hiking with Lone Wolf through the San Jacintos. I predicted I would have the double whammy of having to depend only on my own resources for the challenging high passes while having to admit that the reason for my solitude would be partly my own standoffish personality. (Though once I was complaining to a friend about not being able to get a date and suggested my lack of success was attributable to my poor personality. He unthinkingly replied, "Not at all! Your personality is the thing you have going for you!")

These worries were mild but persistent, so I couldn't have been more delighted than when I came limping into Kennedy Meadows (my blisters worse than ever), to find people greeting me cheerily and encouraging me to go find Lone Wolf, who had been waiting a day and a half for my arrival! I located him in the food tent, where all hikers love to linger. He greeted me with a hug before launching a rapid-fire rundown on how to have an efficient Kennedy Meadows experience.

"First, go sign up for laundry as soon as the store opens," he urged. "Get a shower there too, but you have to sign up for the laundry right away. They only have one washer and people who signed up yesterday afternoon still haven't gotten a load in. Once you do that, come back here and see Dr. Sole."

"Dr. Sole?"

"Yeah, he'll work on your feet. He's in that tent over there."

"Okay, but first explain how I get breakfast!" And soon enough I held a plate of pancakes in my grubby little hands.

After having waited around for me, the well-rested Wolf wanted to hit the bricks first thing in the morning, but I doubted I was going anywhere with my massive blister. Other clients occupied Dr. Sole's tent, so after signing up for laundry, I hobbled over to the store to pick up my parcels, including my bear box.

Through most of Sequoia, King's Canyon, and Yosemite National Parks, the National Park Service requires backcountry campers to keep their food in bear-proof canisters. In years past marauding bears were certainly a big problem, but the parks' insistence on this and other measures seems to have helped a great deal in keeping the creatures wild. Naturally, hikers aren't thrilled about the extra weight, or about trying to fit the bulky containers into our packs, but I only ever met one hiker who didn't acquiesce, and that guy was hiking so incredibly fast that he was only flaunting the rules for just a few nights. I did hear a lot of people speculate that since the bears were now so well-behaved the canisters were unnecessary, but I saw enough bear tracks and scat around the campsites that I suspect it will still be some time before we can forego the use of canisters, and only then if backpackers exercise other precautions.

I limped back from the store to find Wolf urging me to rush straight to Dr. Sole because he was planning on packing up soon. I struggled down to his tent, where he was finishing up his work on Sampson. As we all made small talk together, it came out that Dr. Sole was a retired truck driver who took up foot care when his son hiked the Pacific Crest Trail a few years earlier. In spite of his lack of credentials, the man knew what he was doing. He had a great system for keeping everything clean and sanitary as he popped, peeled, cut, clipped, and anointed our feet. Some people said he must have a foot fetish to be willing to handle scores of such disgusting feet, but it's fine with me if he does, because he certainly deserves some kind of reward for the service he provided! (I actually suspect, however, that his motivation came from Scripture, particularly the part where Jesus humbles himself to wash the feet of his disciples.)

We talked further and soon learned that we both previously belonged to the reform wing of the Teamsters union. We even attended the same convention a few years earlier, and knew all the same people working to bring more democracy and fighting spirit to one of North America's largest labor organizations. The current Teamster president James R. Hoffa (yes, son of that other Hoffa) inspires anger in a lot of rank and file members because he continues to oversee corruption in the union, has failed to engineer strategies to organize new members, and has no substantial experience as a working person. Thus, as our conversation progressed, Dr. Sole grew more and more animated. He spit out phrases like "that damn Hoffa!" Sampson is a hardened Iraq war veteran and an extremely powerful hiker, but I thought I detected a bit of fear creeping into his eyes as Dr. Sole began to wield his needle ever more wildly in and out of Sampson's blisters. I eased us into new topics in order to preserve the state of my friend's feet.

By the time Dr. Sole finished my own feet, I emerged a whole new person. He lanced, squeezed, filed, sanitized, and bandaged or glued everything that needed it. As the very last person he tended before packing up his RV and driving away for the season, I had been incredibly lucky to have squeaked in! Without his care I really don't know how long it would have taken before I could have tackled the Sierras. Even with his excellent service, the largest blister did not fully mend until I was almost to Oregon.

That evening, dozens of hikers converged on the store's bar and grill. Some of us were leaving the next morning, others needed to wait for packages or simply needed rest. I reunited with folks I hadn't seen in some time, and together we cleaned out Kennedy Meadows' entire supply of ice cream. The store sent out for a resupply and we cleaned them out again. We also tore through their inventory of cookies, crackers, peanut butter, and virtually everything else. Managing a store along the PCT must be a very profitable venture when the hikers come through.

Wolf and I set off early the next morning, soon to be joined by Castle and Opus, then later by Heesoo and Sampson, the latter of whom expressed amazement at my gait. Previously, he had only seen me when my massive blister caused me to ambulate with a determined shuffle of sorts. He hadn't realized that I was capable of walking normally.

Almost all the preceding 700 miles had presented dry, desert-like terrain. Now, on the initial climb up to the first 8,000 feet of elevation in the Sierras, a merry brook accompanied us most of the way. Then we lunched by a broad, clear river teeming with trout. Southern California had come to an abrupt end.

We also smelled a forest fire from here. I heard many reports of large fires springing up just behind me, and in some cases the trail had to be closed in sections, but this was the first time I had smelled the smoke myself. From here all the way to Canada, smoke would periodically sting my nostrils and obscure views, although only once would fire force me to alter my route.

The following night the six of us camped with an amusing hiker named Hono who entertained our entire party when he pulled out his harmonica. He also treated us to some songs he had written to the tune of popular melodies. For example, he wrote an ode to his particular brand of stove set to "Clementine." Another tune chronicled his love for his wife instead of "Susanna." The longer we spent away from mainstream culture, the more open we became to this wonderful kind of old-fashioned entertainment. Some recited poetry, some sang, told jokes, or played light-weight instruments. Such people became ever more welcome.

The wafts of smoke continued, but so did the stunning glacial peaks and alpine meadows. Our party now closed in on Mount Whitney—at 14,505 feet, the highest peak in the lower 48 states. En route we joined up with the eccentric Portrait, who had sewn his own pack and spent almost no money as he hiked.

The summit of Whitney does not lie on the PCT itself, but rather requires roughly a one-day detour. Each hiker has their own approach to the trail, but the vast majority decide to attempt Whitney, and of those the great majority succeed.

Wolf was dead set on summiting. Opus very much wanted to, having been prevented from doing so on a previous hike by bad weather. Portrait and Heesoo took it as a matter of course that they would make the ascent. Castle definitely wanted to do it as well, but only if she could summit right at sunrise.

I was the only person in the group for whom the idea of making the trip held no special appeal. The truth is that I don't particularly enjoy the desolate moonscapes of extremely high altitudes. I prefer to see flora and fauna and I find barren rocks rather tedious. However, I probably would have gone along just for the bragging rights if circumstances had been favorable. Instead, as we approached the place where we had to make a decision, dark clouds began pouring in. I didn't have much experience with storms at this elevation and I wasn't sure how nervous to be. Heesoo felt that, while it could go either way, the storm would mostly likely blow over. Wolf, on the other hand, felt that a storm system was settling in for a few days.

Heesoo had more experience hiking at high altitude, while Wolf had more experience living and hiking in California. We all stood around for a long time trying to decide whether to make camp or move on up to a camp closer to the summit. If we camped where we were, it would be much more difficult to summit at sunrise, but a couple of us were quite exhausted and worried about getting caught out in the storm. The longer we stood around discussing it, the colder we became. Eventually, Wolf and I decided to camp where we were while the others went on.

As soon as Opus, Castle, Portrait, and Heesoo departed, I regretted my decision. Wolf still planned to summit, but at this point I struggled mightily with fatigue and I simply didn't want to tax my system any further merely for the privilege of telling other people I had climbed Whitney. If I had gone with the others, I would have been close enough to the summit that I could have given it a shot, but from this campsite I wouldn't attempt it. And so Wolf would take off in the morning and I would again be hiking alone.

I had had enough of hiking alone. In spite of my deep love of solitude, I wearied of not having a second set of eyes to help me assess situations. I was tired of being just one more anonymous hiker in the mass of hikers on the PCT. I tremendously enjoyed this group I had fallen in with, and although they were all a bit stronger than me, I felt that I could keep up with them for some time longer. But instead of sticking with them, I let my crabbiness and fatigue land me in a situation where I would be alone just as I headed into the high passes, which might still be snowy enough to be dangerous.

As it turned out, not everyone in that strong group of hikers made it to the top. Me being by far the weakest of them, I doubt I would have made it myself. Although the storm did pass, as Heesoo predicted, a bitter wind remained that utterly froze two of the four hikers and kept them from reaching the summit. (One of them had loaned her down jacket to an ultra-light hiker with insufficient clothing—he took off with it and made it to the summit while the increasing cold eventually forced her back down.)

As for me, I later heard that Whitney would have been more than just bragging rights. People who made the climb told me that actually it provided an astounding and thoroughly unique view. I feel I cheated myself a bit by not at least trying it.

We had put in some pretty high-mileage days considering the rugged terrain and the high altitude, and I now felt wrung-out. That following morning, for the last time, I would seriously consider quitting the PCT, though for totally different reasons than before. The desert had plagued my nerves with homesickness and demoralizing heat, often leading me to question whether I had what it took to make the hike. But now I had attained one of the planet's truly mind-staggeringly gorgeous places: snow-studded peaks rim clear glacier-fed lakes, which in turn mirror cool skies of faultless blue, while wildflowers, deer, and marmots provide scents and sounds that elevate the spirit. I questioned whether I could do the Sierras justice at the pace I would need to maintain. I thought about just slowing the pace way down so that I could thoroughly enjoy them, even though that would mean I would not make it to Canada in time to finish the trek. Frankly, this would have been a totally sane thing to do, but I am glad I didn't.

Instead, I took one very low-mileage day—only nine miles. That was the lowest mileage I ever did except for when I was coming into or out of a town. I made camp around 1:30 p.m. and allowed the galloping stream running below Mount Tyndall to improve my mood. I sat at the banks, simply taking in the snowy peaks around me. I listened to the birds, I observed the flowers, I smelled the crisp air. I regained a bit of strength. I regained morale.

Still, nervousness hovered when I contemplated the day ahead, which would bring Forester Pass—the most elevated point directly on the PCT. I had taken on a few high passes in the Sierras about 10 years earlier, and one of them had been a perilous crossing. With no hiking poles and an unstable external frame pack, I'd had to carefully traverse about twenty feet of sheer ice on a steep trail. A slip could have easily ended it all. Since then, I had not had the opportunity to do much high alpine hiking to boost my confidence. As I approached my first high pass on the PCT I had the relief of knowing this was a low-snow year, but I still wasn't quite sure what it held for me.

I marched along, alternating between glorying in the beauty and worrying over my inexperience and lack of companionship. I soon approached the nearly 14,000-foot wall of rock that I would traverse via the 13,200-foot pass. But where was this alleged pass? I could see a small notch in the wall, but it didn't seem possible to actually reach that notch. Perhaps I was reading my map wrong or maybe I was looking at the wrong face of mountain altogether.

Another hiker approached. We made introductions and I asked him where he reckoned we crossed. Knut pointed up at the notch. Did he know how we would get there? He managed to pick out part of the trail and I followed the direction of his gaze until I too could see this improbable path. But we still couldn't identify the final stretch of it. He predicted a scramble up an ice-covered wall.

Knut set a jaunty pace while I continued plodding along. The steep, strenuous stretch of trail was not one I would have enjoyed if the snow and ice had been bad, but the ground remained bare virtually all the way up the switchbacks. At the very end, the trail wound through some rocks, which had obscured it from our view when we were below. When I popped out of a chute-like formation to reach the pass, there sat Knut perched on a boulder, scooping Nutella out of a jar with a bagel. I had expected bitter cold winds, but the weather presented calm and sunny, so I too pulled out my canister and began rummaging. We made the requisite jokes about how now that we were at the highest point on the PCT, it was all downhill from here.

The north side of the pass did hold some snow that covered the trail in parts. When we finished eating (not that a hiker ever really finishes eating), Knut and I walked together and found our way easily enough. We were briefly joined on the descent by Scalpel, who confessed that he was afraid of heights and had been terrified the entire way up to Forester. He had a teddy bear pinned to his shoulder strap.

I actually met a fair number of hikers who had a fear of heights. I myself don't exactly fear heights, but I do sometimes get vertigo that makes hiking alongside sheer drop-offs rather unpleasant. We all managed, because we all loved being up in the mountains.

Knut and I continued to Kearsarge, another high pass but this one not actually on the PCT. We had veered off the trail by several miles in order to resupply. In my case, I headed to the town of Independence, whereas Knut needed to take a bus to another town to pick up shoes. We camped that night at a tranquil glacial lake before making our way down to a parking lot the next morning.

Knut hails from Norway, and this fact was a gift for my inquisitive mind. I realized I knew absolutely nothing about Norway. I had gone far too long without a good book, and by now felt utterly starved for information. I plied him with at least a hundred questions about his country, culture, language, and currency. This made the time pass swiftly, and I believe it flattered him a little as well.

My new friend happened to have information that a trail angel was bringing a package to some hikers that morning, so we hustled in hopes of being able to catch a ride back out with him. The switchbacks descended endlessly—at least 60 of them wound back and forth down the mountain. The parking lot came into view a long, long time before we could actually reach it. With a clear view of the road for hours we saw almost no traffic, so we feared that if we missed the trail angel, we would be stranded there all day. By the time we got to the parking lot, I was literally running down the mountain lest I miss the chance to catch a ride. In fact, I focused on my goal so much that I barely registered an oncoming hiker named Train—a tall mustachioed man hiking the trail in a series of 26 wedding dresses. I had heard of Train and been wanting to meet him. I suddenly realized this was him—it was the taffeta that clued me in. "Train!" I hollered. "I love you!"

"Oh, thank you!" he exclaimed. And I heard his receding call, "What's your name?"

"NightinGaiiiiiiiiillllll," I crooned to the air, not knowing whether the sound would reach him.

My prosopagnosia is at least partly to blame for the fact that I did not realize that the hiker stopping to chat with Train was Knut. I couldn't have been more puzzled when he, the faster of us two, came up from behind.

Happily, the trail angel Tom and his faithful dog were waiting in the parking lot and willing to take us to town. In making small talk, we told him about the seemingly endless miles of switchbacks we had just hiked. His eyes scanned the mountain, counting. "Looks like there are about 10," he answered. No, we assured him, the switchbacks went on far beyond those he counted. "I'd say there are about 10," he reasserted. We certainly weren't going to argue with a man offering a ride, so we changed the topic.

Castle, Portrait, and Opus all soon came trundling down the mountain together. They also piled in the back of the truck. Portrait, however, disembarked again when he felt uneasy about the way Tom secured his pack. Portrait, understandably protective of his homemade gear, hitched a ride into town separately about an hour or so later.

As the truck bounced along, I recoiled at the landscape flying by—full-blown desert all over again! Our long descent had landed us back in the hot, scrubby, dusty terrain I had hoped to leave behind for good.

Those of us resupplying in Independence first found a meal and then huddled in the shade of a BP gas station all day while we did laundry and organized our gear. Knut and I made our goodbyes. With some sadness I thought, "Well, there goes a nice guy I'll probably never see again."

I pulled out my cell phone and began dialing the digits inscribed in the case of the sunglasses I had taken from Paws at Walker Pass. I had promised to call Clay, the proper owner, as soon as I could to arrange delivery of the glasses. However, my first guess at the identity of the digits proved mistaken, as did all subsequent efforts. I tried at least seven interpretations of the numbers before running out of ideas. But for the rest of my hike, I would continue to ask fellow hikers if they had contact information for Clay. The next time I had access to internet, I posted queries on the PCT Facebook page as well, but without result.

When the worst heat of the day began to ebb, those of us at the gas station finally worked up the energy to try to hitch the 20 miles back to the parking lot. We stood at a likely spot with our thumbs out. And we stood. And we stood. The hotels were full up due to it being graduation weekend in town, so if we didn't catch a ride we would have to figure out a place to camp and try to hitch again in the morning. Just as we began to despair of our chances, a woman pulled up in a pickup. We recognized her as the waitress from earlier in the day. She was coming back to work now, having been assigned to a dreaded split shift. She told us to wait there and that she would see if it was busy at work. If it wasn't, she would ask her boss if she could run us out to the trail before starting. If she didn't come back, we would know that she hadn't been able to get away.

The sight of her returning truck cheered our spirits. By now we all knew that we had to stay low when riding in the beds of trucks because it is actually not lawful in California to transport humans in this way. When a police car passed us we all held our breath. If we had seen him, he had surely seen us. We hated the thought of this extremely nice woman getting a ticket because of us, though we would have chipped in to pay it. Fortunately, if the cop noticed anything he didn't let on.

As we hunkered down back there, we appointed Opus to be our spokesperson to offer her gas money. We each gave him a few dollars. But when we arrived at the destination, she adamantly refused any cash. That's the kind of generous person I met again and again on the trail. Here was a woman who was not only using considerable gas to drive us to the trail, but was actually missing work to do so, yet even so she would accept nothing in return.

Opus, Castle, Portrait and I shouldered our packs and started back up toward Kearsarge, intending to camp just a few miles shy of the pass itself. Somehow, however, Opus missed the turn-off to our campsite and we didn't see him again until the next morning, when he waited for us at the top of the pass.

Though we wondered where he had gone, we weren't too worried about the competent and resourceful Opus. We made a few forays which yielded no clues, so we assumed he simply had gotten lost in his thoughts and not noticed the turn-off. We each set up our tents. Castle had sewn her own tent. Like many light-weight shelters, it made use of trekking poles for structural support, rather than requiring specialized tent poles. This saved her considerable weight. Castle slept so hard that night, she failed to notice that a deer dragged one of her poles off to gnaw on the salt-soaked handles. Because she finds deer adorable, however, she could not bring herself to admit the nature of the culprit, instead insisting it must have been a powerful mouse.

The four of us re-crossed Kearsarge in the morning to re-unite with the PCT and then carried on over Glen Pass at nearly 12,000 feet. Here we had enough snow that I pulled my microspikes over my boots, while Opus and Castle brandished their ice axes. We could have navigated the conditions easily enough without them (as Portrait did), but Opus pointed out that if there was any question of safety, why not use the stuff that we are carrying? May as well get some use out of the extra weight we lugged up there.

From there we descended into the stunning Rae Lakes basin, full of pristine glacial waters. On our way down we caught sight of a male grouse doing its mating ritual. I had been hearing the thrumming call for weeks, but this was the first time I witnessed one puffing itself up. I must say, if I had been a hen I would have found him quite comely.

The next day we traversed two more high passes, Pinchot and Mather, each above 12,000 feet. By now we all had coughs due to the thin air and I had a lot of congestion that was compounded by the fact that I could not blow my nose vigorously without starting a nosebleed. These problems were further exacerbated by a change in diet leaving me weak.

My bear canister held the smallest amount of food of any I ever saw on the trail. All the hikers had difficulty fitting enough sustenance into their canisters, but size constrained me even more. Actually, not merely size, but shape as well. Most bear canisters are cylindrical, but mine bulges slightly in the middle and tapers at the end—making it difficult for a bear to grasp it, but also difficult to pack food efficiently. On top of that, I am rather zealous on the question of bear safety, so unlike some hikers I don't care to leave anything with any scent outside the canister. Cook set, stove, fuel, bug spray, sunscreen, toothbrush—I want every smelly item except my own person in the bear canister at night.

SHARING THE BACKCOUNTRY WITH THINGS LARGE ENOUGH TO EAT YOU

Some might say I am a bit ridiculous on the topic of bear safety. Yet I know from experience that it is not fun to be the subject of interest to an aggressive bear. I've had numerous bear encounters over the years, but none more memorable than the one in 2007. The summer was hot and I had a new used car. When time came for vacation, I decided to test its endurance by driving from Detroit to the Canadian Rockies.

The weird, possibly offensive, but nonetheless compelling description of my destination in the lyrics of a Gordon Lightfoot song ran through my head all the way to the border:

No one-eyed man can ever get
the Rocky Mountain sunset
It's a pleasure just to be
Alberta-bound.

When I arrived in the town of Banff, I kicked off my hike with a three-day loop that was reputed to provide excellent views. Frankly, it's hard to imagine a trail with only mediocre views out there, but maybe people who aren't from the Midwest have a more finely-tuned sense of this sort of thing.

My first night on the trail, I had to make camp in a crowded site. Several Boy Scout troops (or whatever they call them in Canada) had converged there, as well as a number of families with parents foisting the outdoor experience on their children.

If it weren't for the fact that I had carefully read the park's rules about camping only in designated locations, and if it weren't also for the fact that when it comes to following rules I am more of a Boy Scout than any actual uniformed lad, I would have taken my tent higher up the mountain.

Fortunately, the next morning most parents succumbed to their children's cries for television and descended the mountain. I don't know what happened to the scouts, but I did note the presence of a cliff nearby and didn't ask questions.

Once I hit the trail, I hardly saw another soul the rest of the day. I sang or clapped as I turned sharp corners or crested hills so as not to startle any bears or mountain lions that might not hear me coming—though any wild beast that couldn't already hear me panting like a large wounded animal is probably at an evolutionary dead end. (Because the shrubbery was so much less lush on the PCT than on the trails I was hiking in Canada, I almost never felt the need to take such precautions on that hike.)

So I tread noisily along to the second officially designated campsite, nestled under some pines. A gorgeous alpine meadow rimmed by stunning glacial peaks abutted the camp. I was all alone in the quiet beauty—this was what I had come for. After dinner I gazed out across the meadow and saw what appeared to be a pond at the other end. I thought that if I went over there, I just might see some wildlife as evening set in.

I started picking my way through deer trails in the waist-high shrubs, later identified as blueberry bushes. The evening settled in so still and lovely that I couldn't bring myself to break the quiet by taking my usual precautions of clapping and singing.

The meadow proved many times larger than I had realized and I had walked a good ways into it when I saw a bear running away. I stood there a moment to see if it would reappear and it did.

It eyed me, and I shouted loudly but not—I hoped—too aggressively. I stood tall and waved my hands in the air to look big. Then it stood up and waved its paws in the air, and it looked much bigger.

It dropped to all fours, then stood up again, and then back down. We both repeated our routines for quite a while. At last it started running and my first thought was, "Oh, that's good, it's running away." A moment later I realized that in fact, the bear was running *toward* me.

For just a moment a sheet of white panic enveloped me, but just as quickly I regained control. Now was no time to lose my senses.

I kept my hands high in the air to try to look as large as possible, while keeping my feet firm and square on the ground. I made some more noise without meeting its eyes. With my arms above my head, I felt as if I were inviting the bear to try out the taste of my mid-section, but I couldn't think of a better plan than standing there looking big and difficult to eat. Running would have clearly been a ridiculous choice, as it would have only made my demise more entertaining for the bear.

My mind had selected a point at which the bear was bound to turn around and admit it was bluffing. It ran past that point. Quite a bit past that point. A surprising number of thoughts occurred to me in the next few seconds:

"This certainly is a dangerous situation," I thought.

"Being eaten by a bear will be a truly terrible way to die," I thought.

"What really galls me is that people will say that at least I died doing what I loved, but I will not love being eaten by a bear," I thought with growing irritation.

"I wonder what kind of bear this is, anyway. Before I thought it was a grizzly, but now that I have a frontal view, I sort of think it is a black bear."

This last point was more than a dying naturalist's curiosity, since you are supposed to fight back when a black bear attacks you, and play dead when a grizzly attacks. Though I doubt that in the end it makes all that much difference.

When the bear was much closer than you would ever really want a charging bear to be, it at last stopped and returned the place it had been before. Then it charged again. And again. And to be honest I lost count. I just kept standing there trying to look large and unappetizing, while marveling that this life-and-death situation could really go either way.

When it did stop charging and moved part-way back into the woods, I began to back slowly towards my camp, still a good distance away. It followed me along the perimeter of the meadow for a time, but then seemed satisfied that I was leaving and disappeared.

I returned to camp and wished for whiskey, but had none. There was nothing to do with the rest of the evening except to pretend that I hadn't just been charged by a bear. I tooled around camp for a while, then crawled in my tent. I am blessed with an almost super-human ability to get a good night's sleep, which I managed to achieve that night. I have not, however, forgotten the experience.

***

When I realized it would not be possible to put my fuel, stove, and cook set into the container if I still wished to carry food as well, I had made the decision to give up cooking. When I was at Independence I sent my mess kit home.

Going cookless placed me in the minority of hikers, but there were a few others who didn't cook. Lone Wolf and Knut, for example. I had always viewed this as a peculiarity bordering on barbarism, but in truth the canister constraint was not the only good reason to give up my stove. In years past I thoroughly enjoyed cooking on the trail, but on this trip I had opted for a basically worthless and moderately dangerous alcohol fuel stove rather than one burning pressurized gas. True, my new stove weighed almost nothing, but it took twenty minutes to boil a cup of water. By the time I had hiked 23 miles, I didn't feel like coaxing a meal out of the contraption, let alone doing the dishes afterwards, which was difficult anyway if one wanted to keep a scrupulously clean camp. So the situation with my bear canister was the last straw.

Having rid myself of the cooking mindset, I doubt I will ever carry a stove again for summer backpacking. However, initially I had to figure out the diet, and I wasn't getting it right. I typically eat a pretty healthy array of foods and downright dislike most very sweet items, but when we took our breaks everyone else was breaking out cookies and candy and chips. I came to see the wisdom of this as I feebly gnawed away on my dried apple rings. My last package had contained a small jar of Nutella. Hunger pangs had not reached such a pitch capable of inducing me to eat the stuff, but it turned out to be useful for barter. Most other hikers will do pretty much anything for a spoonful of this chocolate hazelnut spread.

With the altitude, congestion, and inadequate caloric intake, I just barely kept up with the rest of the group. The next day turned very hot, and the heat destroyed what little energy I had. I straggled behind the others, who valiantly waited for me periodically. Each time I came into view, Portrait would examine the appropriate electronic device and reassuringly inform me exactly how many more miles we had to go to Muir Pass, and precisely how much elevation gain it involved. Nonetheless, by late afternoon I was completely wiped out, just as the final major push lay ahead. Reluctantly, I told the others to go ahead, and reluctantly they pushed on.

So often, my lack of confidence became my worst enemy. Muir Pass held the reputation as one of the most difficult of the high passes, not because of its height but its shape. Muir's wide and flat surface holds onto snow much longer than the others and navigation could be tricky as a result. Although all the other passes had been just fine, I stewed over the possibility that I might get turned around in snow on Muir Pass or otherwise run into trouble. I was aggravated

JOHN MUIR

Throughout the Sierras, backpackers encounter numerous references to John Muir, the revered immigrant sheepherder from Scotland who stirred America's conscience toward conservation in the late 19th and early 20th centuries. When not on the Wisconsin farm he called home, he spent countless months wandering the wilderness of the United States, especially the High Sierras. His writing and advocacy were among the most essential factors in the establishment of a mindset that led to national parks, national forests, and other public lands. The famed John Muir trail runs in tandem with the PCT through much of the Sierras. Two lakes in the Sierras are named after his daughters. The gorgeous Muir Pass bears his name. And immediately upon leaving King's Canyon National Park, one enters the Muir Wilderness.

***

at myself for not being as strong as the other hikers, too. I hate being limited by physical inability.

Yet, that night proved to be one of the most beautiful nights of my life thus far. I found a gorgeous flat site tucked into a few gnarled trees. When the sun set, more stars filled the sky than seemed physically possible. Their unintentional majesty nearly hurt to behold. It would take a hard heart indeed not to be lifted by such a sight.

Gaining Muir Pass alone the next day proved one of the best things for me. Yes, the snow still lay thickly, but it was nothing to even begin challenging my capacity. I made a promise to myself that from then on I would stop worrying so much about my ability and just feel good about how much I could do.

Moreover, the pass offered up the stunning sort of beauty which I find most able to absorb when alone. The snowy sweep of landscape was broken only by a picturesque stone hut built by volunteers nearly a century earlier to assist any travelers stranded there in storms. I stood reveling in the entirety of it before descending into the much-famed Evolution Valley.

As much as I loved hiking with Opus, Castle, and Portrait, I felt a great freedom to be hiking on my own again. Yes, I was very weak and moving very slowly, but I didn't mind now because I wasn't holding anyone back. The next 150 miles would see me going happily along at a snail's pace. I still made at least 20 miles per day, I just made them incredibly slowly and I was satisfied with that as long as I was alone.

Thanks to the light snowpack, hiking alone presented no danger. When I forded Evolution Creek later that day, I barely had to roll up my pants. In most years this is a dangerous crossing that could easily sweep a hiker off her feet and down the rushing torrent. In my case, the only negative outcome of the fording was that afterwards I sat on my pack to put my boots back on. In doing so, the bear canister crushed against my water reservoir, popping it. So in spite of an easy ford, my gear got wet anyway.

Losing 1.5 liters' worth of water capacity would have been devastating in Southern California, but in the water-rich Sierras it caused only a minor inconvenience. Instead of being able to draw water to my mouth via the tube attached to the reservoir, I would now have to reach behind me to pull out a water bottle. Hardly an arduous task. My main regret was that the reservoir had been a gift from my sister and I had a sentimental attachment to it.

One couldn't get too upset about such things in the beauty of the valley studded with peaks named after famous evolutionary scientists: Darwin, Lamarck, Wallace, Huxley, Mendel and others. I carried on slowly but cheerfully.

The following day I finally admitted to myself that my frequent urgent need to pee was a symptom of urinary tract infection, and even that sort of cheered me. It provided me with one more excuse as to why I was feeling so dreadfully weak, freeing me from a nagging suspicion that my debility was somehow the result of a character flaw.

Fortunately, by then only one more day lay between me and a bit of rest and laundry. On the morning of June 12, I reached the shore of Lake Edison, where a 9 o'clock ferry would take me to the Vermillion Valley Resort (VVR). I arrived early. Soon other hikers came along as well, including the inestimable Brits and Knut (soon to be given the trailname King Knutella, owing to his excessive love of that hazelnut chocolate confection). Here I also met Collector for the first time, a tall lanky man whose name derived from his penchant for finding various artifacts along the trail.

To my delight, when the ferry docked, Opus and Castle disembarked (Portrait had decided to hike around the lake rather than pay the ferry fee). They produced a twin package of cupcakes they had bought for me at the resort at the other end of the lake. Their plan had been to give it to one of the hikers doing the John Muir Trail, which followed the same route as the PCT at this point. Most of JMT hikers tread from North to South, and we often used them as messengers to people behind us. For example, if we saw a JMT hiker, we might say, "Hey, if you see a tall guy with glasses named such and such, can you tell him that we camped at such and such place tonight?" It wasn't foolproof, but most JMT hikers were happy to pass messages if they could. My friends had decided to ask one of them to carry the goodies to me since they knew I wasn't far behind. But it was better by far to get them directly into my grubby little hands!

Once I arrived at VVR and saw the prices, I realized my friends had gone above and beyond in procuring these snacks for me! This was the most expensive resupply stop on the trail, and with the worst selection. There was some justification for this, however, since the owners had to truck everything in themselves.

As I browsed the stunted aisles trying to piece together enough meals to last me a couple days, I noticed that the bags of chips appeared to have all been opened already, and then taped shut. When I asked the cashier about it, she explained that when they drive the chips up the mountain, the pressure change makes all the bags pop, so when they get to the resort, they have to tape them all shut again. She said it sounds like guns going off in the back when they start popping and that it is great fun to have an unsuspecting new person make the drive.

I spent the day enjoying the company of other hikers. I played chess with Hand Poet and BASA. I consumed one of the best meals on the trail at the restaurant—and reasonably priced too. Then several of us took the ferry back out again that afternoon. Since I was still having to pee about every 10 minutes, Knut and the Brits got well ahead of me that night. The next day Collector caught up and kept me company for a few miles. We discussed Beowolf, Shakespeare, and other literature. Being without books for so long posed one of the real hardships of the trail for me. Whenever I encountered someone who listened to podcasts or carried a book, I milked them for all they were worth just to give myself some kind of vicarious reading experience.

However much Collector may have enjoyed sharing his literary experiences, he could only bear to maintain my pitiful pace so long. By any standard, Collector was a swift hiker, by my standards he was practically a sprinter. So I was soon shuffling along on my own in the glorious solitude of alpine forests.

Suddenly, I heard a woman call out, "Oh my God, I am so happy to see you!" The effusive German hiker Moonshine came rushing up from behind, attempting to execute the impossible—a hug between two people wearing backpacks.

She hadn't seen anybody for days. Her tough, fast hiking style making it hard to find a group who could keep pace with her. In spite of being thoroughly rugged, she had a fear of bears and hated making camp alone in the Sierras. "I'm so glad to see you!" she exclaimed. "Now we can hike together!"

I smiled gamely, but felt pity in my heart for her, since I knew that she was one person I could not possibly keep pace with in my weakened condition. She seemed so starved for company, that I really did put my best foot forward and tried my darnedest. The terrain wasn't too rough, so I thought I might last the better part of the day. Instead, in just a couple miles I stopped for water. When she carried on, I knew I wouldn't see her again for a long time.

This incident captures one of the fascinating traits of the trail. Moonshine had somehow gotten stuck in between everybody for days. Sometimes a hiker can go months at a time just ahead of someone else and never meet them. For example, on the day that I finished the trail in Canada, I met a man hiking south to meet his wife and daughter, a nine-year-old girl named Monkey. The mother and daughter were also finishing the trail that day. I later saw them at the lodge at British Columbia's Manning Park. The entire time I was hiking I never saw or even heard of this girl who broke the record for the youngest person to hike the PCT, though she could not have been that far behind me for most of the trip. Likewise, there was a father/son team I had heard about ever since my first week on the trail. All of my hiking buddies knew them, but I never met them until the final weeks in Washington.

Now I closed in on the town of Mammoth Lakes to resupply, but to get there I would be entering a blowdown area. This section of trail had been a topic of much conversation ever since the previous November, when a massive windstorm ripped through the area. Not only did the Devil's

Windstorm, as it became known, generate 180 mph winds, but the wind came from a different direction than usual. Thus, trees that had grown for centuries accustomed to sturdily resisting winds from the southeast, snapped like matchsticks when confronted with wind hitting them on their weak northeast sides.

Because of the snow at that altitude, no one had even be able to get in to assess the damage until June, let alone start clearing trail. Moreover, much of the damage occurred in federally designated wilderness areas, where only non-motorized tools are permitted for trail maintenance. All of us hikers tried to learn what lay in store for us, but we kept getting closer and closer with no significant information.

The blowdowns posed a potentially serious problem. First, there was the sheer physical danger of getting injured scrambling through layers of interlocking tree canopies. A hiker can easily catch her foot in the crotch of limbs and break an ankle, or otherwise become injured. Secondly, there was the exhaustion factor. How many miles a day could a person manage if they had to climb over huge fallen trees? But most significantly of all, how would we even find the trail if the forest had turned into one massive tangle of fallen giants? Getting lost in the middle of miles of mangled fallen timber was a terrifying thought. All we could do was hope for the best as we neared the hard-hit areas.

The maintainers working this section of trail deserve some kind of trail crew equivalent of the Nobel Prize for what they managed to accomplish. To say they worked hard would be like saying Michael Jordan is athletic. I don't know how they achieved it, but when I passed through, there were very few sections posing any real difficulty. My heart broke, however, as I walked by the sawed-through remains of these trees that had lived as far back as the 1300s. They had taken root before we knew the sun was the center of the solar system, at a time when we were so barbaric we were still fighting wars based on religion and greed. Well, some things never change, I suppose.

I arrived in Mammoth Lakes to find Castle, Portrait, Opus and another hiker sharing a small hotel room. Smelly though I was, even I recognized that this room stank to high heaven like B.O. Nonetheless, I would have happily tried to cram in for the night, except that they were leaving that afternoon. They let me jump in the shower and advised me that Collector and Knut each had a room and would probably be willing to share. Sure enough, I found them both on the second floor balcony, each offering to split the room. I took the spare bed in Collector's room. Later I found out that Castle had told them that I would stay with whichever one of them I thought was cuter, but happily Collector was not the kind of guy to go in for tomfoolery. (Knut later claimed he never heard this challenge, so perhaps Castle was only teasing me.)

Knutella and Collector left together early the next morning, while I hung around to shop for a new water reservoir. If Collector had wanted to win my heart, however, he could have done worse than leaving me his New York Times! Fellow hikers often expressed sentiments like, "Being out here makes you realize what's really important. All that stuff in the news is just a bunch of bullshit stuff to make you worry." But I frankly found the situation in Syria, for example, far more important than my personal odyssey. I greatly appreciated having some access to important events happening in the broader world. (Having said that, one of the great boons of hiking all summer was that I missed the blow-by-blow of the presidential campaigns. I returned home in late October and found that a couple weeks was more than adequate time for making a decision about how to cast my ballot in November.)

By late afternoon I too returned to the trail. During my time in Mammoth Lakes, the mosquitoes must have held a convention and decided that now would be the best time to burst forth from their fetid little lairs. Up until this point, I had been pleasantly surprised at the lack of the beasts, but now they came on in force. They would be a constant presence for the next few weeks, and would intermittently make life miserable almost all the way through the end of the trail.

Other than the nuisance of blood-sucking insects, the trail forged fairly easily onward for a couple days. With mixed emotions I at last crested Donahue Pass, the last of the famous high passes (though there would turn out to be a couple more above 10,000 feet still ahead). I paused to take in the panoramic view on either side. A glacial pond sat prettily in a basin on the north side of the pass, and there I saw a familiar tent pitched on its shore.

Knutella was the only hiker I met on the trail carrying a Hilleberg brand tent. Its sturdy bulk makes it one of the heaviest one-person tents in the backcountry, but that's what one can expect from something designed by the ever-clever Swedes to withstand gale-force winds. Its entrance reminded me of a cave opening. My Norwegian friend hollered out a greeting. The spot was so perfectly beautiful—and had a breeze to keep the mosquitoes away—I considered making camp there myself to join him, but I wanted to get closer to Yosemite's Tuolumne Meadows, where I had a resupply box waiting for me.

The descent held no shortage of gorgeous campsites. I soon encountered Collector's camp. We chatted for a minute and I carried on to some twin lakes I could see below.

I was striding toward another mile-marker of my own— the next morning would mark my 40th birthday. I am not usually a big person for celebrating birthdays, but I must admit that I was hoping that somehow I would have someone to share the day with. I had even let slip the date of my birthday to a few folks in hopes of having some kind of celebration. Still, I didn't expect much—it's not easy to make a special event while backpacking.

Collector surprised and delighted me when he passed me in the morning with a hearty "Happy birthday, Night-inGail!" I hadn't mentioned the date to him, he had heard about it from other hikers. Sometimes it's nice to know one is talked about.

The terrain flattened and I carried along a meadow valley next to a winding river. Within a couple miles of Tuolumne Meadows, I entered a forest where an outfitter led a team of mules carrying supplies for clients. Some of these mules had broken loose and the cowboys and cowgirls were now trying to get the situation under control.

One cowboy secured the remaining animals by tying them to a tree. I wasn't sure how long their leads were so I tread cautiously as they eyed me with the dangerous look of mules who haven't delivered a sound kick for far too long. But I felt much more worried about the ones running around defiantly. I couldn't figure out where to put myself. The mules would gallop down the path full speed until cut off by a wrangler, then they would plunge nimbly into the woods, circle back, and gallop again. I wanted to get through this area as quickly as possible, but I also didn't want to get in the way of the workers or get trampled by the mules as I made my way. So I placed myself next to a tree and waited for the chaos to settle. I figured I'd be able to put the tree between myself and the rogues if need be.

I hadn't stood there long when the mules came rushing terrifyingly right at me—at least that's how it seemed. A cowgirl was close on their heels, in complete command of her speeding horse. She urged her mount onward through the rough terrain, gaining ground on the mules. As she came alongside the lead mule, she leaned way over in her saddle to grab it by its bridle. I'm not sure how she managed to stay astride her mount as she brought the mule toward her and slowed her own horse to a trot, then a walk. I felt like giving her an ovation, but her co-workers seemed to find this to be all in a day's work. "Nice job," the lead cowboy said matter-of-factly as he reassembled the mule team.

My heart still raced as I walked into the Tuolumne Meadows parking lot 15 minutes later. I followed my nose to the knot of hikers assembled at some picnic tables in the shade. Just about everyone I knew was there, and as soon as they saw me they all burst into the birthday song! Then someone produced a cupcake that had been purchased at the convenience store, someone else set a match in it. I blew it out, made my wish, everyone applauded. All in all, one of the better birthday celebrations I've ever had, but it was about to get even better.

The park service permits a vendor to operate a grill next to the store. I stopped in to consume a couple overpriced and overcooked hamburgers, the result of which was that I felt nearly full for a brief shining moment. All the other hikers had taken similar action. Well-fed though we were, we all felt too lazy to push on. I took the opportunity to reconnect with friends I hadn't seen for a while, like Opus, Castle and Portrait, and to get acquainted with people I didn't know.

One such person was the indefatigable Buster, famed for his outstanding singing voice. Since I too serenaded friends along the trail, I always pretended to be jealous whenever Buster's name came up. I would talk some trash about how when I saw him we were gonna have a singing throwdown that would leave him scampering off in the wood like wounded coyote. Now that he stood before me with such an incredibly sweet and friendly demeanor, I couldn't say anything mean to him even in jest. He suggested we find some songs to sing together, and after a few false starts we began to find a repertoire. Knut soon hopped up and joined us as we worked our way through old-time ballads, modern alternative country, and folksy blues. But where it got really good was when Buster started singing the songs he had written himself. With his gorgeous voice, complex yet utterly sing-able melodies, and simple but deep lyrics, I dearly hope we have enough collective good sense as a society to make this young man famous.

While the sing-a-long got underway, Train received his new wedding dress. Many's the time I had thought of him as I worked my way through difficult patches of trail covered with thorns or brush that grabbed even at my hiking clothes. I pitied him for making the same traverse in a flowing gown. Though not all the gowns were flowing. And even ones that might have been longish on the original owner often proved skimpy on his 6′ 4″ frame. The one he picked up at Tuolumne Meadows was a particularly fetching one that flowed behind him.

Who should help him into his new outfit but a young butch lesbian of a hiker? With a cigarette dangling from her lips, she made him gasp with pain when she cinched the laces. They made the perfect wedding party. For days after-wards I would enjoy catching a sight of him striding through the flower-laden alpine meadows in the elegant attire.

Now we all felt festive and feisty enough to consider hik-ing again. Just as many of us began packing up, a van pulled alongside the picnic table. "Anyone want some trail magic?" A young couple with a baby began pulling a large assort-ment of food and beverage from their van. Potato chips, fruit, chocolate, vegetables, beer, pop, juice, cake, potato salad, on and on they placed the spread in front of us.

In spite of the fact that we had all just eaten, we wasted no time tucking right into this largesse. I am ashamed to say I can remember almost nothing about this astoundingly won-derful couple. I believe they had hiked the trail in a previ-ous year and if memory serves they had actually set up shop somewhere farther south along the trail. They had waited for hoards of hikers to descend on them, but by some fluke they didn't meet a single one. So they packed everything back up and decided to drop it off at Tuolumnes Meadows. Happy birthday to me!

At this point our gluttony extended beyond the realm of redemption. We ate with determination, then we ate some more. After a good hour of this, I excused myself for a moment. When I returned, I saw the scene through fresh eyes: A mess of dirty, smelly, skinny people nearly passed out in their food comas still occasionally reached for one more cookie. I felt appalled, but also strangely proud to be affiliated with this group.

The afternoon sun now cast its slanting rays at us, though plenty of daylight still lay ahead. Portrait somehow roused himself enough to push on. He had been hiking with Castle and Opus for a couple weeks now and, understandably enough, had fallen hopelessly in love with Castle. It was an unstated and unrequited love, one beginning to make them both uncomfortable. He now decided to take his leave and resume solitary hiking. He said a fond farewell to Opus, then gave Castle a long, intense hug that one would normally reserve for a soldier headed out to war. I felt for the guy.

The rest of us eventually ran out of reasons to continue hanging around the picnic tables. I set out for the trail alone, but felt more connected to the hiker community than I ever had. I hadn't gone far when first Knutella caught me up, then Opus and Castle. Together we encountered a geological oddity called Soda Spring, which consisted of naturally occurring carbonated water.

We continued chatting our way along the easy terrain. Suddenly, in a wide open spot near the path, we came across a note written in pine cones: HAPPY BIRTHDAY NIGHTINGALE. I challenge you to take the time to gather enough pine cones to spell this out, and you will see what an utterly sweet thing it was to do. But who had done it? I studied the earth around the sign and exclaimed, "Bubble shoes!" Everyone replied, "Oooohhh, Portrait!"

Most of us can't help but memorize the pattern of a few shoes of hikers we get to know. Portrait's left loads of circular marks on the soil, like so many bubbles. He sent my birthday over the top with this slightly misspelled present. It remains one of the best gifts I have ever received on any occasion.

That evening we all camped together at a place called Glen Aulin. From inside my tent, I heard someone approaching. "I almost forgot to give this to you," said a Norwegian voice. Knutella extended his hand. "It's from Collector and me."

I unzipped my tent and opened my palm. He dropped into it an earring with a huge cubic zirconium stone.

"Collector found it on the trail. That's a real diamond," Knutella deadpanned.

"Well, I'm very honored. Thank you." I fixed the earring to my pack, where through repeated applications of duct tape it would manage to stay for almost the rest of the trail. I was within 500 miles of Canada when it went missing.

My journal entries from the next few days are littered with words like "perfect" and "beautiful." Knutella and I hiked together the better part of the time and sang together when we camped at night. In spite of the fact that this was his first visit to this country, he possessed extensive knowledge of American folk songs. As a young student, he had even been part of a band that sang folk songs from the United States, Norway, and other countries.

Our new acquaintanceship was marred only by my getting snippy with him when he did me the "favor" of carrying my pack across a difficult stream crossing. I tend to get vertigo fairly easily, and the condition is nearly always brought on when I need to walk across a narrow log high above rapidly moving water. Just such a crossing set the scene for the incident. Buster and another hiker scampered across with no problem. Then Knut made his way across quite easily. But I was either going to have to crawl across on my hands and knees, or give up on the log and simply ford the creek. I had decided on the latter and began unlacing my boots, receiving some good-natured ribbing from the hikers on the other side. Then Knutella removed his own pack, crossed back, and over my objections shouldered my pack before scuttling back once more to the other bank. Without my pack detracting from my sense of stability, I too made it across the log—though I still crawled on all fours. Knut looked proud as a rooster to have "helped" me in this way.

One thing I really hate is when a man "helps" out a woman simply because she is a woman. I knew he would have never retrieved the pack for Train, Buster, or Opus unless they had specifically asked for help. I've always disliked being treated like I'm incompetent, and ever since I was a teenager I always resented that I was supposed to show appreciation to boys and men when they behave as if I am a weakling.

In my younger days, I used to make an argument out of this sort of treatment, but over time I have come to accept that when men behave like women are feeble, they are just doing their unimaginative best to be a good person. In this case, I was perfectly prepared to take care of my own gear and manage my own creek crossing, as I had for nearly a thousand miles. I reminded myself that Knutella was just trying to be helpful, so I mustered up a thin smile as I took my pack back from him. I was willing to let it go.

Knut, however, was not. He continued to crow about how he had saved me from the terrifying creek crossing. We had developed the habit of making fun of each other pretty much continuously, so he used this as fodder. I managed to bite my tongue until later that day when a small tree lay across the path. He crossed first, then held it down so it would be easier for me to step across. He held out his hand as if he were a footman helping an elegant lady down from a carriage. His expression was one of a man who takes too much pride in this sort of gallantry. I'm sure some women who are reading this now are swooning. I am not such a woman. "Do NOT start doing stuff like this for me," I snapped.

"I'm just trying to be nice," he retorted.

"I know that. Find another way."

One could not list emotional acuity among Knut's many fine traits, for he still lacked the good sense to let the thing drop. He bragged to other hikers about the way he had rescued me and made a royal pain in the neck of himself. At a very small creek he made as if to take my pack. I pulled away and spelled things out for him: "I really did not like that you took my pack before. I did not ask you to take my pack before. You will not take my pack now nor ever again."

At long last, he attained some glimmer of understanding. "You like to do things for yourself?" My affirmative response seemed to clear up something about me he had not grasped and we resumed our amicable companionship.

The hiking now produced few complaints. I had friends to share my experiences. My blisters from Southern California had mostly healed. My bladder infection had mostly cleared up. The weather continued to be good beyond belief. The scenery, incredibly enough, grew only more beautiful. Best of all, my strength returned. For the last 300 miles, I had been exhausted to the point of being downright feeble. But now I grew stronger every day. As Knutella said, I went from being really really slow, to just slow.

I reminded him that he was welcome to take his speedy self farther on down the trail anytime. In fact, his continued presence genuinely puzzled me. When I inquired why he was hiking with me considering how slow I was, he gave me the delightfully candid reply that a man likes to hike with a woman because, even if there nothing between them, it still gives the man status. I must say, this was my first experience with being a status symbol!

The only major annoyance we faced at this time was the ongoing hoard of mosquitoes. Especially in wooded areas, we had to wear bug nets, mosquito repellent, long sleeves, and even with all these precautions, we couldn't sit still or they would bite through our clothes. My sole criterion for lunch spots was whether sufficient breeze could keep the bugs somewhat at bay.

In volume, mosquitoes hold the power to reduce me to the developmental stage of a four-year-old. When they relentlessly bite through layers of clothes and buzz in a thick cloud around my netted head, I WANT IT TO STOP RIGHT NOW! NOW! NOW! NOW!

So it was with an immense sense of dismay that Knutella and I approached a pretty woodland stream, just deep enough to prevent a dry crossing. If we didn't want to drench our shoes and socks, we would have to remove them and wade across. The mosquitoes cackled with glee as we hurried to unlace our boots. Some people on the opposite shore hollered a few questions about where the trail picked up on our side, and we answered as best we could. When we made it to the other bank, we rushed to re-shoe ourselves to get in motion again, our only thought to minimize the insect assault. But these people had other ideas. They strolled up to us leisurely and began telling us all about their hike. They were out for a week and (unfolding their maps to show us) here was their planned route. What did we think of that? And where did we think the trail went from here? We actually weren't totally sure on this point yet. We had moved away from the trail to find an easy place to make our ford and now we needed to cast around to see where to pick it up. But how to politely extricate ourselves from these other hikers?

All along the trail, I tried to conduct myself as a PCT ambassador. I wanted people to have a good impression of the trail, to feel good that their tax dollars support it, and to feel safe and happy around the people who hike it. So I always tried to make time for anyone who wanted to talk, tried to take an interest in their own reasons for being out there. In this particular instance, however, I was possessed by a four-year-old version of myself. I started with the politest answers I could muster through gritted teeth, but as they chattered on I simply stopped answering them altogether. I didn't even make eye contact when I left them standing there with their maps still open.

Based on the few things I gleaned from their talk, they had been in this very spot for hours, even though the mosquitoes receded significantly going either direction on the trail. They seemed inclined to stay there for hours more. The only explanation that Knut and I could come up with was that they had somehow been enslaved by the mosquitoes, and they were required to stand there drawing passing hikers into extended conversations to make them easy prey for their insect overlords. For all I know, they are still there, their speech taking on a slight buzzing quality by now.

Two months of hiking lay behind me as summer came to its height. The Solstice provided one of the most enjoyable 24 hours I spent on the entire PCT. That morning I took my first swim in one of the glacial lakes. Up until now, I had been too cold, too shy, or too attacked by mosquitoes. But at Dorothy Lake a magical wind kicked up just as I arrived and it sent the mosquitoes packing. In spite of worrying about offending the other hikers by stripping down, I plunged on in (leaving on my bra and underwear—I couldn't bring myself to totally scandalize the nice Israeli man named Udi hiking with us that day). The frigid temperature of the water pushed the air out of my lungs and I could scarcely take another breath, but it felt great. I inspired Knutella to take a dip as well.

When we emerged, Knut pulled out a pack towel. As I shivered in the same wind that chased away the mosquitoes, my friend ostentatiously wiped himself dry. I asked him if I could use his towel once he was finished. "No, if you make it wetter it won't dry well." He laid the cloth carefully in the sun with a smirk. If you are now thinking that Knutella must be the biggest jerk you could ever meet, I can assure you I would have done the same thing if the tables had been turned. Sometimes being a snot is the only entertainment available and I enjoyed his orneriness far more than I would have enjoyed the towel.

The Solstice was also the day that I made 1,000 miles. Other than reaching the Canadian border, no other mile marker meant as much to me. It signified that I had made it through the deserts of Southern California, that I had made it through the High Sierras, that I was a real hiker and not some poser. It also coincided almost to the day with the full return of my strength. My urinary tract infection had cleared up for the time, the elevation no longer was such that it debilitated me, and my diet had improved. From this moment on, there would be times when I would be tired and exhausted, but only once more would I feel downright weak.

All day, Knutella and I had been playing leap-frog with Train, Collector, Opus, Castle, Udi, and a guy named Memphis whom I would get to know well in the coming months. Knut and I were bringing up the rear when we hit the 1,000th mile. Everyone had waited for us to get there so we could get a group photo and enjoy a break together. Collector had carried along a small bottle of whiskey to celebrate. Prior to this, he hadn't been inside a liquor store in so long that he had asked the clerk, "Do you have anything in a plastic bottle?"

Feeling good, we set out again, up to the strangely unnamed final pass above 10,000 feet. I can't recall a colder, windier place that a June evening has ever presented me. I hadn't been expecting such a difficult ascent and arrived bedraggled. With the conditions there, I knew we would have to press on still farther to find a place to pitch a tent. I teetered on the brink of surliness. But then Train hailed us from within a small circle of stones arranged as a windbreak for cooking. He informed me that, in fact, we would all be camping right there. "It will be your best night on the trail!"

Memphis and Udi had already counted themselves in; Opus and Castle were not far behind. Although sleeping in the whipping wind and freezing cold was quite obviously a terrible idea, I couldn't have asked for a more scenic way to spend the shortest night of the year. The narrow pass with sweeping views on either side provided the perfect observation point for the sunset and the sunrise that would soon follow. Nobody even tried to pitch a tent in that wind (though Knutella later asserted that the only reason he didn't pitch his Hilleberg was that he didn't want to break the ranks of solidarity).

The sunset did not disappoint. The color spread out across the peaks, tingeing them red and orange, even in the East. Train insisted we all get out of our sleeping bags for a photo and we obliged. He told us to jump in the air at the same time so he could get one of all of us airborne. Then he told us to just jump up and down in as much unison as we could a few times in case the first shot didn't work. Unbeknownst to us, he was actually taking a video of us hilariously trying to coordinate our leaps.

We returned to our bags. When the moon rose, I sang a Hoyt Axton tune about it, then Castle asked me to sing it again, more loudly this time. Still sleepless, Train and I played charades, with the great limitation of not being able to extend much of our bodies outside our sleeping bags.

Eventually, we all settled into our own quietude. Though the cold completely prevented slumber, there are worse fates in life than gazing at the stars for one sleepless night atop a high pass in the Sierra Nevadas.

We rose late that next morning, waiting in vain for a little heat from the sun before breaking camp. Although the temperature eventually became slightly less frigid, nothing like warmth ever materialized. Indeed, the freezing wind continued for miles, accompanied by stunning views as the trail clung to the ridgeline and carried us over a few snow-fields.

My feet felt lighter now that I neared a rendezvous with friends Mike and Margaret, who would pick me up and take me to their friend's cabin near where the trail crosses Ebbetts Pass. To say I was looking forward to this would be a tremendous understatement. Just two days now until I would enjoy their companionship and be resupplied!

Unfortunately, I really did not have two days' worth of food left. Knut noticed the way I was eating sparingly and kept offering me food from his own bag, but I steadfastly lied that I didn't need anything. As hungry as I was, I just couldn't bring myself to mooch off another hiker who had chosen to carry more weight than I had. He nonetheless occasionally thrust crackers or other morsels into my hands, assuring me he had too much. At the time I thought he was just generous; later I would learn that Knutella always carried about twice as much food as he actually needed.

Even with me sponging off my friend, it was going to be a lean couple of days. But somehow on the PCT, whenever difficulties loomed ahead, something always seemed to come up to provide relief. We crossed a road at Sonora Pass that day and as luck would have it, a trail angel had set up shop! We followed his handmade signs to guide us to a shady campsite, where he had cake, fruit, coffee, and tea! This extra bit of food made the difference so that I could eat normally all the rest of the way to Ebbetts Pass.

Even better than the array of food—Portrait was there! This strong hiker could cover a lot of ground, so I hadn't expected to ever see him again when he left Tuolumne Meadows hours ahead of me. After feasting, Opus, Castle, Portrait, Knut and I all left the campground together, feeling very much indebted to the incredibly nice trail angel. Why are people so astonishingly kind to hikers?

The only unsettling development was the presence of signs warning that rodents in this area carry the plague. Obviously, this is an unfortunate circumstance and I'm sure no one was particularly overjoyed to see the notices, but I had particular cause for concern. Two mornings earlier, I had broken camp and made my way down the trail. When a bit of thirst tapped my shoulder, I reached for the mouth-valve attached to my reservoir of water. When I sucked on the valve, I noticed it felt a little funny. I pulled it out of my mouth and gave it a once-over. Rodents had been chewing on it. Now, I know I should have stopped using it and switched to a water bottle. But I figured that since I had already used it once, I may as well just go with it. I rubbed a little water around the valve and wiped it with my pretty disgusting shirt and resolved not to think too much more about it. These plague warnings had me imaging the conversations I would have with family and friends as I made my final goodbyes. "Yes, I know I shouldn't have kept sucking on something that rodents had been gnawing on, but, well, it was just more convenient…"

Happily, the particular rodents that nibbled on my water valve didn't appear to be carrying the plague. Or else there is a long incubation period.

We hiked as a group for about 20 miles, at which point Knutella said he was feeling a bit tired. We stopped for a break, planning to catch up with the other three to camp. Our break nook had a good spot for a couple tents and a tolerable view. Knut suggested we just call it a day. As usual, we ate dinner then perched on some rocks and sang together while the sun set. By this time we had gotten pretty used to each other, and I wasn't looking forward to losing track of him when I got off the trail to visit my friends, but I didn't say so. He broached the topic, suggesting that he should hike a few short days so that I could catch up with him at Echo Lake a few days past Ebbetts Pass. That was an agreeable plan to me, and when he reached for my hand, that was agreeable as well.

When I started the trail, I had considered the possibility that I could find someone special, but pretty quickly ruled it out. Nearly everyone else on the trail was about 20 years younger than me, and the remaining demographic was about 15 years older. Knut was 13 years older than me, but he moved with the agility of a much younger man. I figured I'd just go with it.

The odd thing was that, although laughing together was one of our strengths, the first moment our lips met I felt a great wave of sadness. Something important about my hike was coming to an end—my being completely in charge of my own comings and goings. I didn't know how long Knut and I would continue hiking together, but now that our relationship was changing, that's how long I would be beholden to another person to a certain extent. I knew how to hike my own hike, I wasn't sure I would know how to hitch my hike to someone else's. Still, I had sense enough not to sit there and stew over all the what-ifs when I had a perfectly lovely man offering to bring a new sense of enjoyment to the hike. Some of my fears would prove well-founded, most would not, and none of them would have justified rebuffing the advances of someone I quite liked.

Thus it was that when I arrived at Ebbetts Pass, I was in even higher spirits than I already would have been to meet up with two people I am beyond proud to call my friends. Bizarrely, I arrived within 45 minutes of the time I had suggested to them as a possibility when we first talked about meeting months earlier.

I made the acquaintance of Mike and Margaret when I lived in Detroit. They have since moved to Richmond, California, where they live extremely busy lives of contributing to efforts to bring some justice to this world. Even though Margaret was scheduled for surgery in just two days, they made the long drive out to pick me up, drive me around to get groceries and other items, took me to a coffee shop where I could check email, then brought me back to the cabin to cook for me. In short, they treated me like royalty. They even brought me Epsom salts so I could soak my feet, which had recently seen a flare-up of blisters.

I cannot describe just how rejuvenating it was to be physically taken care of. But better still was their companionship. I had met a number of wonderful people on the hike, but almost nobody with whom I could talk in an in-depth way about my values and beliefs. We could talk about political strategy, opportunities for changing the world, and our socialist leanings. Being able to share my true self with this couple healed something more important than blisters and reconnected myself with the part of me that the other hikers didn't see or engage.

I spent less than 24 hours with these fine people, but when they dropped me off at the trail again the next morning, I felt completely rested. I picked up a six-pack of pop to leave at the trail to surprise the next few hikers passing by. It felt great to finally give a small amount of trail magic instead of only being on the receiving end all the time.

I was now due for a day of solitary hiking again. I simply love being alone in the wilderness. I love stopping in my tracks to listen to birds or to the silence. I love experiencing the hike on my own without trying to keep up with anyone else. The most surprising revelation the PCT awarded me was that even more than the solitude, I love having a good hiking companion. Still, the chance to have a few days on my own lightened my heart.

Along about late afternoon, I met a hiker coming the other direction. Billy Goat is something of a legend on the PCT. This septuagenarian spends months on the trail every year, going where he pleases without worrying about doing the whole thing. He might do one stretch 15 times if he likes it and he can tell you all about the flora, fauna, and history of those places. He might rarely or never visit sections that don't suit him. This was my second encounter with him, though due to my problem with recognizing faces I didn't realize until later whom I had been talking to.

He looked wiped out. "I think I'm done for the day," he said. "The wind up there on Nipple Ridge is not safe. Don't go up there today if you can help it."

If I had known this was Billy Goat, I would have taken his advice more seriously. As it was, I thought he was someone out for just a few days, someone not used to the typically strong winds that can rip across the ridges. The fact that he looked so wiped out fed my incorrect belief that he probably wasn't in very good shape.

I came to the cusp of the exposed traverse of Nipple Ridge in early evening. The place is named, by the way, after a peak that indeed looks just like a nipple on a well-formed woman's breast. By now, the wind really was quite strong and I could see that it would not be an easy jaunt to get across this exposed, steep, scree-filled ridge. When I came to some level ground sheltered by large boulders, I knew this would be my last chance to camp. The sun was sinking low already, so I could either stay there and get across the ridge in the morning when the wind would likely be less strong, or I could forge ahead. Usually, I tend to err on the side of doing what is easy and sensible, but my spirits were high and my body felt strong. I pushed on.

I hadn't experienced winds like this since Tehachapi. Once more, gales buffeted me about like a pinball. Sometimes they knocked me off my feet. I was into my 22nd mile for the day and losing steam. But with no place to rest, I had to push on to try to get across while I still had some light. Throughout the ordeal, I could see a sheltering forest on the other side. I just kept creeping along toward it.

By the time I reached that forest, the sun had set. Even down among the trees, the wind hardly abated. I crouched behind a rock and began pulling out dinner items. Bear canisters were no longer required by law, so I had left mine with Margaret and Mike to send home. Tonight I would need to hang all my food in a tree. For now it was in a nylon bag inside my backpack. Imagine my dismay when I reached into it and felt something oily.

I had purchased some almond butter whose oil had separated out. The container had leaked and now almond oil was working its way steadily through my backpack. With frozen hands, I did my best to wipe it off my clothes, sleeping bag, and tent, but wiping oil off fabric is, in fact, not possible without detergent. Hanging my food now seemed rather silly since I would be climbing into an almond-flavored sleeping bag, but I figured that if I survived the night then I should give my food the best possible chance of doing the same. By the time I found a tree to hold my food and managed to tie it up there, my hands were completely numb and still the wind howled.

I found a low area just sheltered enough to pitch a tent and stay a little warm. Nonetheless, I scarcely got a wink of sleep due to the unceasing wind that tore into the trees and whistled across the rocks. By morning, the wind had still not calmed to a great degree, but by pressing on I was soon out of its reach.

That day I crossed Highway 88 at Carson Pass, named after famous mountain man Kit Carson. A small information center lies there, the staff of which kindly gave me a tangerine and an apple. I later learned that if I had arrived one day later, I would have found it staffed by the ex-wife of a good friend! She had been keeping an eye out for me. The parking lot also had a monument to Snowshoe Thompson, an eccentric Norwegian-American who for 20 years delivered the mail without any compensation between Placerville, California and sites in Nevada. He actually made use of skis, but the local people had no frame of reference for this Norwegian device and referred to his skis as "snowshoes."

The following morning, I cruised into the parking lot at Echo Lake—a small resort on a large lake. Like most hikers, Knut had hitched a ride from here to the town of South Lake Tahoe. Virtually all hikers take a zero day there to rest up from the High Sierras, deal with details like shipping off their bear canisters, and resupply. Since I had been able to do all that with Mike and Margaret, all I needed to do was pick up a package I had sent to the resort here and wait for Knut.

A terrific surprise awaited me when I went to pick up my parcel. Not only was there my own package, but packages from my mom, my aunt Ruth, my friend Anusuya, and friends Ken and Martha. There were also letters from a number of friends, several from my dear friend Jessica.

Without Jessica, I likely would never have been able to complete the PCT. She is an active outdoors person herself, and was utterly committed to helping me succeed. In fact, sometimes she seemed even more committed than I was. If I needed something shipped to me, she figured out how to do it. If I needed a shoulder to cry on, she was there to provide it. If I wanted an audience for my latest misadventure, she gave me her ear. I hope that before it's all said I have been that kind of friend to her as well.

With my haul of packages and letters, this unemployed woman felt like the richest person in the world. I picked through my loot, sharing with the other hikers resupplying at Echo Lake. I ordered breakfast at the grill, and shortly followed that with first lunch. After second lunch, I was ready to move on again. I left a note for Knut telling him what time I was leaving and estimating where I would camp that night. I knew he wouldn't have a problem catching up with me.

As it turned out, he arrived at the resort only minutes after I left, so we were soon reunited and singing our way down the trail once more.

We camped that night above 9,000 feet at the wide and flat Dick's Pass, which afforded 360-degree views. We tucked ourselves well off the trail in a copse of trees. Here, grouse pecked their way along the ground as the sunset colors consumed the sky. The beauty of the place filled me with so much energy I started turning cartwheels until I was too dizzy to keep it up. "That thing you just did," Knut uncharacteristically failed to find the proper English word, "I cannot do that." I tried to entice him to give it a try, but he felt that a remote mountain pass was not the place for a grown man to take up gymnastics.

This burst of energy carried me all the way to Donner Pass, a few days down the line. Here, I would be meeting my friend Ron, who works as an Amtrak engineer in nearby Reno. He and I had gotten to know each other through some work I did with a group called Railroad Workers United.

RWU draws its membership from the array of railroad trades (conductors, signalers, track maintainers, mechanics, engineers, dispatchers and so forth). Railroad workers suffer a despicably high rate of workplace injury and death, they often have crazy schedules that virtually ensure dangerous fatigue, and they are fighting off attempts to strip crews to just one person. These men and women are the unsung heroes who move massive amounts of freight and passengers as safely as they can through your town. RWU works to make sure they can do their jobs without losing their own lives or being party to an accident that costs someone else's life. Until I started working with this group, I had never realized just how many train accidents are occurring out there. Ron himself had, almost exactly one year earlier, been the engineer on a train that was struck by a gravel truck. One conductor and four passengers were killed, as was the truck driver. He and others at RWU have long pushed for safer crossings, so this was a disturbing and ironic tragedy. I hadn't seen him for years and couldn't wait to give him a tremendous hug.

Donner Pass is such a pleasant, accessible, and popular spot, that it's hard to believe it was once the site of unimaginably brutal suffering on the part of emigrants who only kept themselves alive through cannibalism. Instead of being victims of hunger that day, Knutella and I were beneficiaries of some trail angels who had set up shop there. I ate first lunch while I awaited Ron's arrival.

In chatting with the kind folks who grilled up hotdogs for us, I learned that the Supreme Court had just declared Obamacare constitutional. I had been away from the polarized nature of public discourse for a long time and felt some fear now about what these folks might say. I dislike the Affordable Care Act because I believe that health care is a human right and ought not be one more way for insurance companies to turn a profit. I also dislike the law's requirement that people purchase a product on the open market. To my mind, it would be much better to have the government provide the service, and if a person chooses not to avail themselves of it, that is their right. In spite of my dislike for the legislation, I also dislike the way most other opponents characterize it. Whereas I believe that health care is a fundamental right, many opponents believe people who get sick at the wrong time have only themselves to blame and deserve whatever life-altering or life-ending complications might ensue.

When the topic came up, I dreaded what I might say if this kind and generous couple would be opposed to health care for all. I feared my inability to keep quiet about my views would put me in an awkward position as someone at the receiving end of their hospitality. The hosts, learning that Knut was Norwegian, began asking him questions about how socialized medicine worked in his home country. I can honestly say I was shocked by their curiosity. For more than two years, the only time I heard anyone on any side of this debate ask a question about health care was when they were trying to score points. But lo! Here were people honestly trying to figure out what kind of system works! Knut answered candidly, talking mostly about how well the Norwegian medical system works, though also pointing out a few problems. I found myself cringing as he mentioned the problems, wishing he would only talk about the positives. In doing so, I realized how I myself had become part of the polarization plaguing our country. I turned off the point-scoring part of my brain and tried to listen more honestly. I am still trying to live by this lesson.

When Ron pulled up in his trusty old pickup, I was so happy I could have eaten him up! Knut and I agreed that while I spent the day with Ron, he would carry on at a slow pace and I would hike double time to catch up to him the next day.

Before I loaded into Ron's cab, he escorted Knut and me to a monument near the back of the parking lot. This stone slab commemorates the Chinese labor that had done so much to build the railroad running through the pass. He pointed at the base where the name of the group that built the monument was inscribed: E. Clampus Vitus. "I'm a member of this group, I'll tell you about it as we drive."

So I said goodbye to Knut and climbed in. I asked Ron to take me to the nearest restroom before we set out, and he obliged. I did my thing and got back in the vehicle. Ron gave me a funny look. "Don't take this the wrong way," he said, "but have you always walked kind of … um … different?"

I laughed. I had forgotten about the hiker waddle. We backpackers get so used to having the pack on our backs that when the weight is lifted we have sort of have a hard time remembering how to walk properly. We also often have blisters, bruised feet, or other pain that gives us an unusual gait. I explained this all to him. "Well," he grinned, "it looks kind of badass."

Back to The Ancient and Honorable Order of E. Clampus Vitus. As I understand it, this is a fraternal society that mostly convenes for the purpose of drinking, but sometimes gets around to putting up markers of historical significance. Start looking at some of the historical monuments you see, especially in California, and you will notice that some of them were erected by Clampers. Don't bother trying to research the history of this group, the members specialize in distributing playful fictitious accounts of their origins. However, to hear Ron tell it, the organization originally began in the mining camps of California in the 1840s. Some guy invented it as entertainment and diversion. Their mission was "to take care of the widders and orphans, but especially the widders." The group more or less died out, but somehow got revitalized in the 1960s and is growing. Its name is fake Latin and doesn't mean a thing.

Ron brought me out to his cabin home on the Truckee River. His joy at seeing me evaporated completely when I removed my boots. "Those are going outside. Now." Even I could hardly stand the stench of my boots and feet, so I didn't need any persuading. As soon as they were safely outside I washed my feet to get the worst of the stink off of them, then covered them up with clean socks.

After I cleaned up still more, my friend took me to the Reno train station, where I got a ticket to ride Amtrak's California Zeyphyr, while he climbed in the engine to take me and fellow passengers to Winnemucca. I watched the cactus fly by the window, secure in Ron's competent hands.

When he completed his shift, we met at one of many Basque restaurants in the town. Basques immigrated to this part of the country in some number beginning in the gold rush of 1849 and mostly ending in reverse migration shortly after World War II. The descendants of these immigrants know how to put on a good meal for tourists like me. I cannot imagine how anybody who was not hiking the Pacific Crest Trail could even begin to put away all the food presented to us. I ate so much I disgusted even myself.

We were accommodated in traditional Basque seating of long tables with multiple groups sharing the space. The father/son duo next to us struck up a conversation and by way of apologizing for eating like a barbarian, I explained that I was hiking the PCT. These two were also avid hikers and we chatted for a bit. When they got up to leave, the father laid $60 on the table and told me to use it for dinner or whatever else would help me on my way.

This kind of generosity never ceased to amaze me. Something about my rather selfish trip inspired a lot of people to acts of kindness. For my part, rightly or wrongly, I had early on decided to never let pride keep me from accepting these gifts. Instead, I thanked the man sincerely and had the privilege of buying dinner for my friend instead of him picking up the tab as he had planned.

As with Mike and Margaret, I reveled in being able to talk to a friend who shares my values, works for similar goals, and is damn smart about how to do it. But as much as Ron and I enjoy talking politics, we usually get around pretty quickly to prognosticating on the topic of the bizarre thing called love. We never have quite figured it all out, but sometimes after a few beers we come pretty close. Our best thinking on this topic might be summed up by the Mae West quote Ron used to keep taped to his mirror: "Marriage is a great institution, but I'm not ready for an institution."

In the hotel that night, we puzzled over what to do with my boots. The stench would have prevented my friend from getting a decent night's sleep—something important to his role as the engineer ferrying passengers back to Reno the next day. Yet he feared that the boots might be stolen if left outside the door. We tried putting them in a drawer. Ron endured for a time, but even I could tell the stench filled the room. I felt pretty confident nobody would be stealing them and pitched them outside.

Upon return to Reno, Ron hauled me back out to the Donner Pass to hike with me the first few miles north from there. I tried to convince him to quit his job and come along with me to Canada, but he apparently has just barely enough good sense to avoid such a fate. We said our goodbyes and I pressed on to catch Knut.

Unfortunately, within a couple hours I fell victim to the Revenge of the Basques. I won't go into great detail, but I will simply say that I am glad I had packed plenty of toilet paper. Instead of going more than 20 miles as I had planned, I made it only seven miles. Toward the end of the day I ran into a couple other hikers and asked them to keep their eyes open for Knut so they could let him know I would be behind schedule.

By the next morning I felt fit as a fiddle and hit the trail early, trying to make up lost ground. Before long, I was surprised by the sight of Knut coming down the trail toward me. He had gotten the message and left his pack at camp to meet me. Now he attempted to carry my pack for me until we got back to his own, but I really was fine at this point and insisted on carrying my own weight. He definitely scored some points for coming to meet me, though. I like to think I would have done the same thing, but it's not easy to decide to backtrack towards Mexico when you are trying to get to Canada. It made me think that maybe this guy really did like me.

We made good miles that day, ending up near campgrounds on Jackson Meadow Reservoir. We paused to get some water at a stream near a road. A passer-by saw us and stopped her station wagon. "Do you guys want to come to my cabin?" PCT hikers will never answer no to this question. The result was a wonderful evening in a tent next to her cabin on a lake that offered a gloriously refreshing swim. This woman turned out to be a wonderful person who gave us food, built a fire, and played her accordion for us, but to be honest, we would have climbed into the car with pretty much anyone.

Now I was becoming practically spoiled, because the very next night after accepting this kind woman's hospitality we came to the small town of Sierra City, where we met up with the Brits and Memphis, among others. Breakfast in town included homemade biscuits and gravy, which gave me so much energy that I actually led the pack the next day, wearing out my friends. The only times I ever outpaced anyone was coming off a town breakfast.

As it happened, this was Independence Day. I am not nearly the most patriotic person you could ever meet, but I couldn't resist the opportunity to annoy my British and Norwegian friends by singing all the patriotic songs I could summon. This in spite of the fact that in the eyes of passers-by I was fast becoming Norwegian myself.

It seemed whenever Knut and I met day-hikers they would ask us where we were from. I would reply "Wisconsin" and Knut would reply "Norway." We would chat for a bit, he in a Norwegian accent and me in generic Midwestern tones. Yet later we would encounter other hikers saying something like, "Oh you must be the Norwegian couple those day-hikers told us about." One gentleman even informed me that I had one hell of an impressive American accent!

My ability to annoy my friends with patriotism had not achieved the desired level most of the day. But things really got good when we camped with Memphis that night and he began reciting great national speeches: the Gettysburg Address, the preamble to the Constitution, the Declaration of Independence and so forth. Neil (the male half of the Brits) kept muttering "Tomorrow will be the fifth. Tomorrow will be the fifth." Thus reminded that we only had a few more hours to press our patriotic spirit, we merely ramped up the singing and oratories.

We were now making our way to the town of Belden and the end of the Sierras. But first, I had one more trailside visitor. My oldest brother Ray lives in the Bay area and found the time to drive out to meet me for a day, bringing with him the most amazing array of food and drink. We went to a nearby park and spent the day hanging around a shady campsite with his guitar. He and Knut took turns playing and I sang along. When the afternoon nudged toward evening, we parted, but I first took some of the beer Ray brought and left it as trail magic for hikers coming behind.

From there came a gorgeous stretch of trail that ended in a beautiful but scorching descent into odd Belden, which turned out to be my least favorite place on the entire trail. The heat suffocated, and on the Sunday morning when we arrived, a rave was wrapping up. I like electronica, but not early in the morning. Still, I would have admired the zany costumes many of the young people were wearing, but I was too disturbed by the vacant looks on the faces of these folks wandering around stoned on something that didn't look like much fun.

From there we walked along an oven-hot road to the house of some trail angels. When we arrived, overheated hikers already lay sprawled on every bed and flat surface. Usually hikers welcome each other heartily and create a festive atmosphere, but this time people barely mustered a grunt and a wave. The kitchen suffered from sloppy-man syndrome, and I couldn't find the resupply package I had shipped there. On top of that, Knut and I bickered uncharacteristically. All in all, an unpleasant day.

By the time we started the 5,000-foot climb out of Belden, we were more than ready to be on our way. It was an inglorious end to what had been an absolutely glorious passage through the Sierras. The volcanic Cascades range lay ahead.

Northern California

B iscuits and gravy once more fueled the climb. With protein, carbohydrates, calories and lots of fat, this traditional American fare is pretty much the ideal way to launch a new stretch of trail. Plus, it always brings pleasant memories of my father—the designated chef when the situation called for the dish.

As we made the ascent out of Belden, volcanic rock displaced the Sierra Nevada's granite while the elevation gradually dissipated the oppressive heat. When curiosity drove us up a side ridge we found such a perfect view that we permitted ourselves the luxury of a short day.

One of the downsides of hiking the PCT is the relentless pace I had to set—or sometimes merely convinced myself I had to set. If I wanted to make it to Canada, I would need to average about 20 miles per day. Since resupplying entailed short-mileage days, that meant I needed to do more than 20 miles most other days. As a result, I rarely sat for more than an hour except to sleep at night. So to spend the final six hours of daylight doing nothing but enjoying the fact that I was in the wilderness with Knut made for an exceptional day.

Thirty-five miles north of Belden, a small marker declared we were now equidistant between Canada and Mexico! I arrived at the marker ahead of Knutella and found fellow hikers Salty Snacks and AquaMan celebrating by calling friends and family. Rarely could I find a signal in the wilderness and I would not have even thought to turn on my phone if they hadn't been there chatting away. While I waited for my friend, I gave Jessica a call to announce the news.

"What is that racket in the background?" she asked. "I can barely hear you!" It was AquaMan.

Salty and AquaMan made an unusual pair. While Salty Snacks usually said positive things when he spoke at all, AquaMan talked a great deal and at great volume. The latter didn't shy away from saying cruel things about people or from advertising his own great accomplishments. The duo shared the ability to push themselves to the limit with long, hard days and I suppose that was partly why they kept hiking together. You could never run into them without Aqua-Man regaling you with one of his outlandish feats such as the time he hiked so long and hard that he passed out, foaming at the mouth (he made this sound like an accomplishment instead of foolishness). The funny thing was, no matter how fast they hiked or how many miles they covered, I kept seeing them. I guess their exploits left them so exhausted by the time they got to town to resupply that they needed to recuperate a bit longer than the average hiker. But however much I would have disliked this style of hiking for myself, I came to appreciate that everyone has his or her own manner of doing things. I expect they would have been bored out of their minds to cruise along with my relatively low-mileage days.

Knut soon came trundling down the trail. We all took pictures, congratulated each other, and dispersed a few platitudes about how it felt to be halfway to Canada before we moved on down the line to Lassen Volcanic National Park.

Mount Lassen's 1915 eruption sent a tower of ash 30,000 feet into the sky and spread debris 200 miles. Avalanches, floods, and mudslides decimated the area around the volcano. The contiguous 48 states wouldn't see anything like it for another 65 years, when Mount Saint Helens erupted in Washington. We had already been getting terrific views of impressive Mount Lassen for days, now we were treated to one of its boiling lakes! Few things thrill me more than glimpses into the weirdness of geothermal activity lurking beneath the surface. I could have stared at this steaming, stinking lake all day if not for the call of the one thing that thrills me even more—food.

The park is home to Drakesbad Guest Ranch, a wonderful resort resting in a wide valley. From there, guests can take horseback rides, swim in the hot-spring-fed pool, and eat at the excellent restaurant. The owners are kind enough to let hikers ship packages here, use the showers, and do laundry. But best of all, they feed us! They, quite understandably, seat hikers at a table rather removed from their other guests since at this point it would have taken more than a shower and fresh clothes to wash the stench off of us. After having served their regular customers, they brought us a stellar meal of turkey, mashed potatoes, green beans, and lasagna at only half the cost.

That night we dined with some section-hikers as well as the British couple Neil and Tanya. Upon learning it was Neil's birthday, Knut and I ordered a carafe of wine to celebrate, only to find out that Neil is not much of wine drinker. While he bought himself a beer, Tanya, Knut and I managed to figure out what to do with the wine.

The Brits had taken a side route earlier that day to see the Terminal Geyser. (It actually isn't a geyser at all, but rather a fumarole—essentially a steam vent in the earth.) They pronounced it as "Terminal Geezer," which provoked an entirely different image in my head. I normally don't make fun of people's accents but in this case ... what am I saying? Actually I do. I am terrible. I make fun of people's accents a lot. But you shouldn't. It isn't nice.

Back on the trail, the renewed heat somehow seemed fitting for travel through the volcanic terrain. At a café near the crossing of Highway 44, we waited out the hottest part of the day with the Brits, Memphis, and a section-hiker named Eric. We were all about to embark on the last of the difficult waterless stretches—Hat Creek Rim. As often happened during the second half of the PCT, the conversation drifted toward The Next Big One. That is, the next long distance hike we would each do. Memphis had already completed the Appalachian Trail. Knut and the Brits had hiked through the Himalayas and Pyrenees. One trail we all agreed we'd like to try is the Continental Divide Trail. It also runs from Mexico to Canada, but further east through the Rockies and roughly 400 miles longer than the PCT. The CDT is more remote and more difficult, especially in terms of navigation. I felt rather honored that these seasoned hikers asked if I'd be interested in doing it with them in a couple years. Somehow I had developed a sense of myself as the weakest hiker in any group, so I always felt surprised to be considered an asset.

We had one more stop to make before climbing Hat Creek Rim—Subway Cave. Molten lava that cooled more quickly at the top than the bottom created this cave. As a ceiling formed from the hard cool lava, the molten lava kept moving through, eventually emptying out the tube. This long multi-branched tunnel stretched about a third of a mile and required the use of our headlamps. After making a tour, we sat in the cool chamber near the entrance, waiting for the searing sun to descend a bit more before heading out to the waterless, shadeless rim.

Knut and I left first. Although the rim lifted us only another 800 feet, it opened terrific views. Most people consider this section one of the worst days of hiking on the entire PCT, but thanks to the fact that I was able to do the first part as the day was cooling and to accomplish most of the rest of it the next day before it got too hot, I immensely enjoyed its finer points. In fact, with receding views of Mount Lassen and the first views of Mount Shasta, Hat Creek Rim proved unspeakably pretty.

The soft colors of the fading day still provided enough light to see the clear bear tracks on the trail. I had told myself that this barren area wasn't likely bear country and that I wouldn't need to bother with a bear hang in that treeless plane, but clearly I had been wrong. The most common large mammal on the rim, however, was cattle. Like much of the public land in the West, the government opens the area to ranchers for grazing. The only problem this really posed for us was that we couldn't find a place to lay out our sleeping bags that didn't have cow patties. They are mostly just pooping out cellulose, so I tried not think about it too much as I spread out the tarp and sleeping bag.

I loved those nights that we skipped the tent to camp directly in the open air. The stars above me, the breeze on my face, those first rays of light, all of these things made me feel that I was just exactly where I wanted to be.

I rose in the predawn light and broke camp while Knut still slept. We had an arrangement whereby I would typically start hiking before him. That way I usually had an hour or two of the solitude so vital to my sanity. Also, Knut tended to hike faster than I cared to in the mornings, so it allowed us each to go at the pace we pleased. The trail that morning ran along the west side of the rim, permitting me the longest possible period of shade. Partway across the rim, a trail angel had left a few jugs of water. As kind as this act was intended, the water appeared to be stored in poorly-rinsed milk jugs, so I refrained.

By the end of the afternoon, Knut had rejoined me and we had descended back down from the rim through stark red lava fields. We still hadn't hit the next water supply point when we came across a leaking aqueduct, squirting cold water straight in the air. The shocking sensation put us in such a good mood that we stopped to play a little king of the mountain on the pipe—miraculously ending the game before either of us suffered an injury.

Around this time I took to making random bets with Knutella. I'm too embarrassed to relate the content of all the bets here but let's just say that for some reason I believed that female elk have antlers. When we got to the next resupply point at McArthur-Burney Falls State Park, other hikers noticed me making good on the bets by buying pint after pint of ice cream for my smug companion. Smelling something fishy, they succeeded in learning the details. I tried to redeem myself by relaying stories of my elk encounters, including the time I heard one make a kind of eerie laughing sound. This, however, only increased the ridicule from the crowd. A few days later I found that one of these hikers had mockingly scribbled "Laughing Elk" into the dirt where he knew I would soon be passing. I know if I hadn't already had a trailname, I would have been stuck with that and everyone meeting me for the first time would have imagined I thought myself so spiritually deep as to deserve a faux Indian name.

But the ridicule was okay, because at Burney Falls State Park I had something even better than ice cream—a visit with my friends Ken and Martha! These outstanding people didn't even live anywhere in the vicinity. They had come to California from Detroit for vacation and borrowed a friend's car to swoop down on me and Knut, whisk us off to a nearby town, and put us up at a historic hotel. These pals share my enthusiasm for backpacking, worker rights, science, and good conversation. We discussed botany, ornithology, history, politics, and even a little gossip before they deposited us back at the trail the following morning. If you want to find out who your friends are, hike the Pacific Crest Trail.

Before we said our goodbyes, we stopped to educate ourselves using the interpretive signs at the park. The volume of water moving down the falls shocked me since Burney Creek had been dry when I crossed it just a half mile upstream. By reading the signs, I learned that the water percolates down through the volcanic rocks that make up the creek-bed, meaning that much of the year the creek is running underground, emerging just in time to make the 130-foot plummet down twin falls.

Mount Shasta loomed ever larger as we parted company with Ken and Martha. The route around this most gorgeous of mountains is one long detour. The direct thing to do would be to head due north, on the east side of Shasta. Doing so, however, would expose hikers to far too much risk. Most thru-hikers traverse this region in mid-July when the rain-shadowed expanse to the east of Shasta is barren and dry to a seriously life-threatening degree. Thus, we take a long route, first heading almost due west, then north, then east again. This results in Shasta as a constant presence for hundreds of miles, with hikers still catching glimpses of it well into southern Oregon. The lush country we ranged through easily merited the extra mileage in any case. Much of Northern California along the trail grew rich with lilies, lupine, larkspur, Solomon seal, and other flowers. Even the occasional forget-me-not still stood remindingly near lakes or streams.

And speaking of lakes, around this time we took one of the loveliest and littlest detours of the trip. One fine afternoon a small sign pointed us toward Red Mountain Pond, if we should care to leave the trail for a moment. One couldn't possibly stop to make every side trip along the PCT and we weren't due for a rest break, but for whatever reason we decided we'd pop over to the pond, which we encountered in less than 50 yards. This delightful little body of water hardly held more volume than a large puddle. Within, dozens of newts swam around doing whatever newts do—thriving at it, in fact, as far as we could tell. This may not seem particularly noteworthy, but for me the wilderness is less about the sweeping vistas than it is about getting these occasional glimpses into some newt-shaped little world. I love to stare for long periods at tiny tucked away niches and marvel at all I will never know.

As we moved into late July, we began to be overtaken by "the herd." Nearly everyone with whom I had been regularly hiking had started in mid-April. Most hikers, however, don't start until late April, with hundreds beginning immediately after a large kickoff party the last weekend of the month. As I understand it, gear companies show up, various groups do education, and nearly everyone gets drunk. Then the backpackers start their hike. Up until now we had managed to stay ahead of the herd, but now faster ones overtook us in waves. Previously, upon meeting a new hiker, we'd all make introductions and ask for news about who was ahead or behind us. But now, we just stepped aside and let people through. This wave only lasted a few days, and the next wave didn't hit us until the week we made Canada, though naturally we continued to be passed by strong hikers all along.

We now entered parts of California much less well-known than the Sierras or Shasta, but so rugged and wild that I wished I had a full summer to stay within just one of the areas like Russian Wilderness, Emigrant Wilderness, or Marble Mountain Wilderness. Before passing through these beauties, we came to the Castle Crags, whose ragged peaks delight the eye. If a Midwestern state had a jewel like this, we'd call ourselves "The Castle Crags State," but in beauty-drenched California many people born and raised in the state have never even heard of this park. In fact, it had even been threatened with closure in a recent round of budget cuts.

We had hoped to resupply at the small town of Castella near the crags, but the convenience store was bereft of anything of interest to a hiker (except very friendly staff). On top of that, one of my packages hadn't shown up yet—the one with my two person tent. After about a month of hiking together every day, Knut and I had made the risky decision to combine a little gear. I asked my house-sitters to send me my light-weight two-person tent, which they promptly did, but the mail moves slowly out of my small town in northern Wisconsin.

We hitched a ride into the town of Mount Shasta, where we got a room and did our laundry. In fact, we did such a thorough job of drying our clothes that nothing ever quite fit the same afterward. My hat in particular took on a unique and un-headlike shape. I kept wearing it, always assuming I would find another one in a hiker box. But none turned up and by the time I reached Canada I wouldn't have traded it away for anything. After our zealous laundry experience we went out to a restaurant, where I had the pleasant experience of being carded. I decided that it must only be because I looked like an undercover cop.

Back at Castella the next morning, we had a brief encounter with Moonshine, my friend who had been so ecstatic to encounter me after days of solo hiking in the Sierras. I hadn't seen her since then, but instead of stopping to chat, I had to rush into the post office to check once more for my package before it closed for the weekend. She was gone by the time I emerged. I assumed I would see Moonshine again sometime when her swift strides would bring her past us farther up trail. That didn't happen, but we stayed in touch after the hike and when I found myself in Istanbul not long thereafter she connected me with a friend who was studying there. Both Moonshine and her friend were German Turks and architects who knew the city well. I promised to someday venture to Berlin to see them both. Yet within a few months, Moonshine had died, a victim of suicide. I can't bear to omit this truth nor can I bear to make a platitude-laden transition to the rest of my story, so I ask the reader to take a moment to honor this fact in some way of your own choosing before rejoining me on my hike.

Knut found a lovely creekside shortcut which eliminated a couple miles of hot road-walking. Before ducking into the woods for his path, however, we feasted on the huge blackberry bushes swelling with roadside fruit.

The next several days brought us some of the most varied and stunning terrain we'd had. The countless miles of chaparral in southern California and even the endless snow-capped peaks and glacial lakes of the Sierras could sometimes produce a feeling of monotony in me, but now the landscape changed regularly, from the cragginess of the Castle Crags, to the stark rounded tops of the Marble Mountains to the sprawling ruggedness of the Russian Wilderness to the perky but distant views of the Trinity Alps, every day brought something new. We saw pitcher plants (carnivorous moisture-loving fellas), rattlesnakes, snowfields, wild strawberries, thimbleberries, and one morning I crossed an incredible wide grassy pass with dozens of raptors on the prowl in the winds above. Another morning a deer ambled down the path toward me. Even after it saw me, it kept strolling my way. Steep scree surrounded the narrow path on either side, so although one of us was going to have to move, it wasn't going to be me. It finally began picking its way up the side of the mountain. I felt bad to see that it was having a bit of trouble getting its footing, but the sight did also make me feel a little better about my own habit of losing my balance.

In addition to the beauty we did have some things working against us. The mosquitoes for one thing—or should I say for millions of things? I challenge Creationists to defend their position when it comes to the mosquito. For another thing, some days the forest fires that were springing up behind and around us created an impenetrable wall of haze that obstructed views. On the physical front, my urinary tract infection flared up again.

Knut had some concerns of his own—mainly the boots he had picked up from Tanya at Drakesbad. She had new boots shipped to herself there but her old ones still had quite a bit of life. Knut's were falling apart and the two hikers wore about the same size, so he swapped out. We didn't see the Brits for some time after that, but as per usual whenever we saw other hikers we would ask for news of any of our friends. We started hearing that Tanya had a rather awful fungal infection on her foot!

When we finally ran into them again in Oregon, Tanya immediately pulled Knut aside saying, "There's something important I have to tell you."

"I already know, and I don't seem to have caught the infection," he replied. If you didn't know the back story, you would have imagined a different sort of scenario than an exchange of footwear. I also developed a weird foot problem that produced big sunburn-like blisters on the tops of my toes. For some reason, I insisted that sunburns was exactly what they were, though of course my feet were always inside boots. I simply chose not to believe that I, too, had a fungal infection of some sort.

Whatever problems we developed, at least we weren't peeing blood like our friend Memphis. I rather worried about him when I heard this news and urged him to take a couple days off the trail to rest up. He decided to keep going however. Eventually he caught up with Running Wolf, who is a physician in real life. Running Wolf told him that it's not actually that uncommon and that he should focus on staying hydrated. The human body starts to do funny things after you've been hiking awhile.

And we certainly had been hiking awhile — 1,600 miles of trails lay south. On July 29, we made our last pit stop in California, at the town of Seiad Valley. Some people claim that at this point we had already crossed state lines — into the State of Jefferson. Seiad Valley lies in the heart of a propagandistic secessionist attempt that flared in 1941, when local residents, frustrated by lack of infrastructure investments, took control of a part of Highway 99. They drew on more serious efforts to carve a separate state out of Northern California and southern Oregon a century before.

On December 4, 1941, they began collecting tolls from the drivers passing into their "state," handing out their proclamation in exchange. Throughout the region, supporters posted signs such as

Our roads are not passable,
hardly jackassable;
if our roads you would travel,
bring your own gravel.

They generated plenty of attention—for three days. Then, on December 7, Japanese forces bombed Pearl Harbor and the country had more important matters to attend. Secessionists put aside their claims as the country mobilized for war. In Seiad Valley, however, the post office still identifies itself as part of the State of Jefferson, and the "state" logo (two X's on a gold pan to symbolize the double crossing of the region's populace) can be seen on various signs.

For hikers, this small town is known for one other reason—the pancake challenge. The café there will, if asked, serve up a plate of pancakes so big that the person who eats it all can have it for free. In years past, this was apparently doable by the very determined, but from what I understand, relatively new owners have since increased the portions and now even the most famished hiker wouldn't be able to achieve it. I did not make the attempt and the omelet I ordered instead was absolutely scrumptious. As was the second one I had a few minutes after devouring the first.

By the end of the day, we began the 5,000-foot climb out of the valley, putting less than two days between us and the officially-recognized state of Oregon. As dusk encircled us, we began to worry about our prospects for finding a spot flat enough to pitch a tent. Other hikers had veered off the path to camp near an abandoned firewatcher's cabin, but we

THE PROCLAMATION HANDED OUT TO STOPPED MOTORISTS DURING THE SECESSIONIST MOVEMENT IN 1941

You are now entering Jefferson, the 49th State of the Union. Jefferson is now in patriotic rebellion against the states of California and Oregon. This State has seceded from California and Oregon this Thursday, November 27, 1941. Patriotic Jeffersonians intend to secede each Thursday until further notice. For the next hundred miles as you drive along Highway 99, you are traveling parallel to the greatest copper belt in the far West, 75 miles west of here. The United States government needs this vital mineral. But gross neglect by California and Oregon deprives us of necessary roads to bring out the copper ore. If you don't believe this, drive down the Klamath River Highway and see for yourself. Take your chains, shovel and dynamite.

Until California and Oregon build a road into the copper country, Jefferson, as a defense-minded State, will be forced to rebel each Thursday and act as a separate State.

State of Jefferson Citizens Committee
Temporary State Capital, Yreka

***

didn't feel like adding to our mileage so we had pressed on. As the sun started to sink, we came across a small saddle with just enough space for one tent. The big red orb spread its rays all around the snow-capped volcanic peak to the west and reflected off the giant orange moon rising in the full east. Two tired hikers removed their boots and climbed into their sleeping bags.

OREGON

I'm not sure what we were expecting at the border between California and Oregon, but the crossing didn't live up to it. I suppose after nearly three and a half months through the long wild Golden State, we somehow imagined we'd be welcomed into Oregon with a brass band or something. Instead, it was just one more hot, nearly shadeless line through a day of hot, nearly shadeless hiking.

On top of this, Knut felt unwell. He carried a heavy pack and didn't much care for long days, whereas now that I was recovered from my Sierra slowness, I tended to want to push myself. For the longest time I thought he was just trying to be chivalrous by "offering" to stop so that I wouldn't have to make the request myself. Lately, however, my cheerful insistence that I was perfectly happy to carry on for miles yet was being met by a silence stony even by Norwegian standards. As we moved toward the resupply stop of Ashland, Oregon, I still didn't really understand that we might have an underlying issue. Both of us, however, looked forward to a well-deserved zero mileage day in Ashland. Even with all the visits and resupply stops I'd had, I had still hiked at least a few miles every single day since leaving Tehachapi nearly 1,200 miles ago. Knut had not had a zero day since waiting for me near Echo Lake more than a month earlier.

In a field of wildflowers just before reaching Ashland, we ran into some day-hikers. One of them asked if we had a place to stay in town and invited us to stay with her and her husband on our second night in town. She gave us her phone number and we parted ways, with Knut and I marveling once again over the kindness of strangers. It's really a wonder things didn't turn out better for Blanche DuBois.

Hitching a ride to Ashland the next day involved sticking our thumbs out at an entrance ramp to Interstate 5. Usually when we needed to get to town we were along small highways where all the locals know that giving a lift to hungry hikers means that they are not only doing an incredibly kind deed but also depositing someone in their town who is likely to contribute to the local economy without causing too much trouble. In general, people hiking the PCT have a pretty good reputation as responsible, respectful, and eager to spend at the local cafés and grocery stores, and hotels. But to the interstate traffic, we were just a couple of dirty stragglers with large packs. We stood in the wilting heat for nearly an hour. I still gave my most winning smile, but it was becoming rather less winsome with each passing car.

At last a maroon station wagon pulled over. A kind young man said he'd be happy to take us into town, though he'd be taking back roads if that was okay. We piled in. He and his mother had hiked about half of the PCT together during a previous year, so he knew how much it meant to us to be picked up. The car wound farther and farther into the hills following ever narrower roads. He turned onto a dirt track, saying that he just needed to stop at his uncle's. Being in the middle of nowhere with a stranger who is bringing you down a dirt road to his uncle—well it's the kind of thing that probably ought to raise a few red flags, but I never could seem to muster enough anxiety to properly worry over the motives of trail angels. And once more my trusting instinct was rewarded.

When we arrived at his uncle's landscaping business, the driver had us wait near the car while he checked on a few items. In a little while he returned and told us he actually had to go back to work now, but that his mother would drive us the rest of the way into town. Before long, she approached us, obviously having come from a shift of good hard physical labor. It's easy to feel like a slouch around landscapers.

Our joy at resuming our trip to town diminished only slightly with the mother's decision to roll up all our windows. At first I thought she was doing it so that she could turn on the air conditioner, but the a/c stayed off. I'm sure there was some very good reason for this, and she was probably so used to taking this action that she was immune from the heat-trapping effects of the glass windows, but by the time we reached Ashland, our faces were pretty pink. I suppose it only added to our anticipation of the upcoming day of rest.

I was particularly looking forward to this day, because it was here that I would get to meet Jessica.

The last several months comprised the longest period of time Jessica and I had ever gone without seeing each other. When we met up in Ashland, she administered a crushing hug, and since she had just come off of a backpacking trip herself, I didn't even feel that guilty for smelling so bad. (Though there was a crucial difference between us—she was able to smell okay again after a shower, whereas at this point my stench was deeply embedded in my skin and my clothes.)

We left Knut to contemplate some purchases at a gear store and headed out to find lunch with Castle and Portrait. Yes, Castle had texted me to let me know they were in town too. I was surprised, however, to find my two friends walking hand in hand! So Portrait had finally won her heart after all. I couldn't have been happier for them. They told me that after the last time they had seen me and lost me again near Ebbetts Pass, they had bought a candy bar for me and carried it 300 miles to Hat Creek Rim, where it melted and Castle drank it.

I was less happy for myself when I arrogantly challenged Jessica to an arm-wrestling match. This skinny little woman is tough as nails, but I thought that finally I would be strong enough to take her on. You can imagine how pleased with herself she was after beating me soundly. "You actually made me work for it a little bit this time," she quipped smugly.

From there we scooted over to the library so I could get online. When the library closed, we scooted back out again. On the steps I ran into Frost—the only hiker I had met in the first 100 miles that I still saw frequently. Frost had received his trailname on the Appalachian Trail due to his memorization and recitation of the poems of Robert Frost. I previously asked him if he knew my favorite Frost poem, "Out, Out—" but he hadn't heard of that one. I had just looked it up and written it down in anticipation of our next meeting. I now whipped it out of my pocket and recited it for him. (Look it up yourself, it's quite a poem!)

Jessica hiked with us a few miles after driving us back to the trail, then left us to our final six weeks of hiking.

The next morning, I set out on my own as usual, anticipating that Knut would catch me before long. A few miles in, I found a sunny meadow and decided to have second breakfast while I waited for him. I had intentionally selected a stump sized for not one but two butts, yet when he arrived at the clearing he pointedly sat away from me, barely returning my greeting.

Trepidatiously, I approached to ask if something were the matter. He retorted that he was sick of me driving him at such a pace. He was plain tired.

I hadn't expected this after two restful days in town. I'm not sure why I was feeling so strong compared to Knut at this point. He was solid muscle and I frankly was not. But he carried a very heavy pack, even by my standards. The only thing I could think to do was to take some of his weight.

We had previously divided up the weight of tent we shared, but now I pulled the part he was carrying out of his pack and placed it in my own. He was either too grouchy or too sensible to object. We hiked surly and separately until lunch, at which point we got bored with being mad at each other and made up. But this issue of pacing would come up for us again and again nearly all the way to Canada. Two middle-aged people used to being alone can find it a challenge to suddenly start accommodating each other.

Speaking for myself, my ability to be reasonable was not increased by the hordes of mosquitoes. And we were about to make a decision that would plunge us even deeper into their bloodsucking realm.

The PCT used to follow the Oregon Skyline Trail before being re-routed some years ago. The OST is now little-used, but there are a few places where some guidebooks recommend taking it as an alternate route. We approached an intersection with one of these alternate routes. Staying on the PCT supposedly would mean no views and no water according to one guidebook, whereas the OST supposedly had lovely views and lots of lakes. So we opted for the OST.

Lots of lakes meant lots of mosquitoes. And really, the views were nothing to write home about. Later we heard from other hikers that if we had stayed on the PCT for this stretch we would have been treated to one of the singly most gorgeous days of the entire hike. We heard others raving about that stretch of the trail for weeks to come.

Our mosquito-infested OST included a six-mile walk on a paved road. I don't do roadwalks if I can help it. Road-walking gives me no pleasure and doesn't really count as "trail" to me. Therefore, when I could hitch a ride for those few short sections where the trail was routed on a road, I had no objection to putting out my thumb and hoping to catch a ride. Knut, on the other hand, wanted to have continuous footsteps across the country. He didn't care whether every footstep was on the official PCT, he just wanted to have an unbroken line that he had walked. So when a car pulled over to offer a ride, I hopped in and took Knut's pack as well. The woman drove me the six miles to Lake of the Woods Resort, where the trail re-entered the wilderness.

I decided I would surprise Knut by being less mileage-driven and rent a cabin for the night. Until I looked at the prices. My next step was to look into a canoe rental for the day and found that prospect to be more in my budget.

I ordered second breakfast at the restaurant while I awaited Knut's arrival. After I scarfed down an omelet and home fries, I checked my cell phone and was delighted to find that I actually had a signal. I wasted no time in dialing up my friend Scott. In the course of the conversation it came up that apparently I had at some insane point informed him that I would be at Crater Lake sometime around the last weekend in July (it was now early August and I wasn't quite there yet). As a surprise, he had rented a yurt near Crater Lake, planning to take me there for a little off-trail wilderness relaxation.

Although I am not normally a flaky person, for some reason I have given Scott a lot of bad information about my likely whereabouts over the years. During an earlier visit to Oregon, I had told him I would be on the coast and he planned to rent a yurt that time too, but I was actually nowhere near the coast. I'm lucky he has such a high tolerance for my flaws. Fortunately, his rented yurt near Crater Lake did not go to waste as he took his girlfriend Meghan there for a mini-vacation.

The PCT creates fertile ground for missed connections. Many people sent me letters and packages that I never received and a number of efforts to visit people living nearby failed. Sometimes it was because I got ahead of or behind schedule. At other times it was because I couldn't get a cell phone signal during pertinent times, or because shipping destinations' level of chaos prevented me from locating parcels. Many places along the trail allow hikers to receive mail, and some of those places have an organized system for allowing that to happen smoothly. Others simply toss each new package or letter into a corner and let hikers root around to find what they can.

When Knutella arrived, tired but cheerful after his hot six miles on the road, he ordered up his second breakfast, then we headed out for an afternoon on the lake in a canoe. I paddled while he lounged in the front, serenading me with Bob Dylan songs, Norwegian folk music, and more. Then he paddled while I serenaded him with Gillian Welch songs, American folk music, and my own material. We swam a bit before returning to the restaurant for dinner. We looked through the board games they had on a shelf and played chess over our hamburgers. When we finally ventured back in the woods that evening, we felt rested and happy for each other's company again.

The next day we left the Oregon Skyline Trail behind to rejoin the PCT at the first opportunity. I wouldn't have traded that afternoon on the lake for anything, but we were eager to get out of the mosquito-ridden basin and into Crater Lake National Park. Shortly before we arrived, I had my first confirmed sighting of a marten. I thought I had spied them once or twice darting across the trail, but never had a proper look at one until one went racing by us in pursuit of a squirrel.

Martens look a bit like a cross between a ferret and a fox. They once thrived back home in Wisconsin but due to habitat loss and trapping, they went extinct there in the late 1930s. They were reintroduced in the 1950s without success, then again in the 1970s and '80s. We now have a breeding population, but they continue to suffer from habitat damage. Tribal and state authorities are attempting to protect some of their ecosystem in hopes they will make a comeback.

At Crater Lake we stopped first at Mazama Village, where we did laundry, grabbed a shower, and picked up my resupply box. Best of all, Knut reunited with a crew he had hiked with through part of Southern California and the Sierras. Just as I always asked other hikers for news of Opus, Portrait, Castle, Supergirl, Little Bear and others, this entire time that I had been hiking with him, Knut had been asking people for news of Gourmet, Peru, Gutsy Rabbit, Moose, and Scalpel—collectively known as Team All Dead. Each of these hikers had started out separately, but formed a group that made it all the way to Canada. At times the group expanded, for example when Knut was hiking with them, and at times it shrank when one of the members might go off trail for one reason or another, but this core group of five more or less stayed together starting from somewhere in the first 600 miles.

I have already introduced a couple of these hikers—such as Rabbit who had been carrying her pet mouse until, shortly before Crater Lake, little Ella had somehow gotten out of her cage. Also, Scalpel was the young man I met coming down Forester Pass, the one who was afraid of heights. Peru was the botanist who had put me in my place at the Andersons' in Southern California. Gourmet is a professional jazz musician and producer whom I had met at Donner Pass, and I had also met the quiet, kind expert angler Moose then.

The whole crew had, for all this time, rarely been more than a day's hike ahead of or behind us. Gourmet announced that his partner would soon be meeting them to treat them to a week of slackpacking, and that we should get in on it. (Slackpacking is when someone else transports your heavy gear by car, and you cover the miles with just what you need for the day.) It was hard to say whether our schedules would coincide enough to make it work, but we were certainly grateful for the offer Gourmet extended.

By mid-afternoon we left Mazama Village to head out for the magnificent lake itself. En route, I ran into Portrait, who gave me the unfortunate news that Castle was running a fever. They had been camped out nearby for a couple days while she attempted to recover. I bought a vitamin water at the store and asked him to take it back to the tent for her with my wishes for her health. I felt so relieved to later learn she was up and around again. These two hikers made Canada together and the following year completed the famed Continental Divide Trail. Since they both had already completed the Appalachian Trail, they are now in an elite group of backpackers who have hiked the Triple Crown of North American long distance hiking.

Crater Lake is the seventh deepest lake in the world, and as a result of that depth, all the colors in sunlight are absorbed except for the most intense blue you could ever hope to see. The water rests in the caldera formed nearly 8,000 years ago when Mount Mazama blew its top. Over time, the hollowed out mountain filled with rain, which now evaporates at roughly the same rate as it accumulates.

We reached the rim of the caldera just as the heat of the day wound down and the colors of sunset ramped up. The time we spent walking along Crater Lake was without a doubt, the most photograph-intensive hours of our time together. Even I took at least a dozen photos with my disposable camera, I can't begin to guess how many Knut must have snapped through his digital lens.

This section of trail presents challenges to the faster hikers, who find much of it under heavy snow when they come through early in the season. But for us the PCT was in perfect shape for enjoying this phenomenally beautiful lake by the time we arrived.

In spite of the vast quantities of water resting so beautifully below, the next easily accessible source to hikers was not for another 27 miles. Fortunately, Knut had talked to a trail angel who had just left a water cache near the PCT about 10 miles into this waterless section. We were lucky to have this intelligence, because we would not have found it on our own. The angel had left the water on the equestrian route, which at that point diverges somewhat from the more scenic route most foot travelers take. Moreover, the angel had wanted to keep the water tank shaded and thus covered it well with a brown tarp and some leaves. Only Knut's sharp scouting located it. Once we took our own water, we made an arrow with sticks and wrote "H20" in the dirt. When we returned to the main trail, we left a note under a rock to provide directions to other hikers.

Still riding high from the majesty of Crater Lake, we quickly came upon Diamond Peak, with its snow-covered image

HIKER COMMUNICATION

One common way to communicate with hikers behind you on the trail is to leave a note under a rock with most of the paper sticking out. We get so used to seeing only natural things, that the note catches hikers' eyes immediately. Of course, if you leave a personal message, you have to accept that every person between you and the intended recipient will also read it, but that's the price one must pay. For example, Frost once left a note for Memphis explaining that he uses a pee bottle rather than get out of the tent in the night. This bottle had leaked in his sleeping bag and drenched everything in urine. For that reason, he would be delayed in meeting them at a previously agreed-upon site. Another time, Knut left a note for me which was signed "KKK." This apparently means something different in Norway than in the United States.

In addition to notes for specific hikers, one from time to time leaves notes of general interest to any hikers, such as "water is this way," or "there is a nest of bees on the trail ahead."

***

reflecting perfectly in the still waters of Diamond Lake at its base. From there we pushed on toward needle-shaped Mount Thielsen, standing high and alone on a scree-filled ridge.

A side trail branches off for those who care to summit Thielsen. An assortment of hikers rested near the junction. We all sat around eating and gossiping and trying to persuade each other to go on up there and climb Thielsen. None of us took up the challenge, though I later heard from Memphis that he and the Brits had bagged the peak in what turned out to be one of his favorite days of the trek. Instead, we walked on through a haze of mosquitoes which, against all laws of nature, attacked us in the midst of a smoky haze. With fire season now in full swing, smoke filled our nostrils most afternoons.

The fires might have obscured our views, but couldn't dim our spirits, especially when Gourmet's partner Jayne and friends came down to meet him. As Gourmet had promised, they brought trail magic and they offered slackpacking. Best of all, Jayne brought Gourmet's saxophone. When he put the instrument to his lips and began to play, he wore the expression of a man deeply in love. Prior to starting the hike, he had played almost every day since adolescence. The hikers assembled around the campfire that night were treated to the real privilege of a professional making music sound like the force of nature it is.

Jayne ferried our gear 30 miles or so up trail to Shelter Cove Resort that night, and I hiked with only the detachable top compartment of my pack that doubles as a fanny pack. Knut had a storage bag with some small shoulder straps for his daypack. Everyone else just removed the heaviest items from their packs and used their regular bags. After hiking for so long with about 40 pounds on my back, I suddenly seemed to have helium attached to my body as I glided along.

At the end of the day, we found Jayne's campsite. Not being sure how many of us could camp there without paying extra, we tried to be low key and figured it would be easier to beg forgiveness than to ask permission to have us all on site. Most of us didn't pitch tents that night, instead sleeping in the open air. At some point shortly after dark, a neighboring camper came by and made a scene about the fact that there were so many of us at the campsite. I slept through the whole thing and didn't hear about it until the next morning.

When day hit, Knut set off on foot to walk about two miles of pavement before the trail tucked itself back into the wilderness again. I waited for a lift, along with those of the Team All Dead who either had already hiked that section the day before or who were fine with skipping it.

The process of arriving at the trailhead provided a challenge to my rigid personality. I come from a large German Catholic family parented by people who used orderly and organized systems for things like chores, meals, and transportation. They expected my siblings and I to be where we were supposed to be a few minutes earlier than we needed to be there—or else. The lesson stuck. So when someone says they plan to give me a ride first thing in the morning, I am up and ready to go with everything packed.

I loitered near the car after saying goodbye to Knut, expecting the loading of the vehicle to shortly commence. A few details came up for others that needed to be taken care of before we could leave, and of course some people were slower than others to get ready. All of that's just par for the course. Then the campground store opened and that provided more opportunities for malingerers to poke around for snacks and coffee. I kept checking in to see what the scheduled departure time was, trying not to sound pushy but also wanting to be sure that I wouldn't be the person to hold up the process.

As the delay lengthened, I hung around the shop, as any self-respecting hiker would. At one point I was standing at the counter with Scalpel, who suddenly started talking to the cashier about the conflict the night before. We had been in the right, he asserted, and the neighboring camper had been in the wrong regarding how many people were camped at our site.

Although I did think our neighbor overreacted, considering we were quiet and respectful when the sun was up and sound asleep as soon as it set, I wasn't totally sure we were actually in accordance with the resort's regulations on this point. It seemed to me that the less said about it, the better.

Scalpel, however, was determined to set the record straight. "We paid for that site!"

The cashier was clearly hearing about this for the first time. "Which site is it you're talking about?"

"Oh, don't worry about it," I chimed in. "It's a site over there, I don't remember the number, but it all got worked out."

Scalpel persisted. "Site 22. It was paid for by..." And he spelled Jayne's first and last names. "They said that we had too many people on the site, but we paid for it."

The woman turned on her computer. "Well, let me look it up for you."

I jumped in again, "There was just a little mix-up. It all got taken care of by the guy on duty last night. Hey Scalpel, did you know they have bacon burritos here?"

"Mmmm ... bacon ... can I have one of those bacon things?"

The woman turned from her screen to give him an apologetic look, "I'm sorry, I don't have access to look up the information about your campsite right now, but I can get you your burrito." She reached into a freezer and tossed a cylindrical food-like substance into the microwave. "I can go get my supervisor and she can look it up," the clerk offered.

"No need! It was all taken care of already!" I assured her. As soon as I could I ushered Scalpel out of there and back to the campsite, where the imperceptible process of packing continued.

Knut had left around 7 that morning. The clock now pushed 9:30 and folks still sort of milled about making some idle talk about departure. I finally started to get tense and even grouchy, then I checked myself. Here were these people who were letting me tag along for some slackpacking even though they barely knew me. And what Jayne was doing for me was really above and beyond. It might seem like no big deal to just tote our backpacks to the next point up the trail, but 25 miles by trail might involve 60 miles of driving on hard-to-find dirt roads. And in that sparsely populated region, if she needed to go to town for gas or supplies, that might take her another 40 miles out of her way. On top of that, if we left anything behind at the camp—as had happened the first day, it was up to her to load it into the very full car. So I gave up being annoyed and just laughed at myself for being way too attached to punctuality, especially when I had no clock to punch or schedule to keep.

Eventually, everyone seemed to be packed and ready. The campsite looked clean and tidy. I thought we hovered on the brink of departure and went so far as to stand up and put a hand to my bag. Then somebody looked around and asked, "Does anyone else want a cup of tea?"

"Only if there is some peppermint left," someone replied.

Thus began unpacking and rooting around in the car to produce a stove, a pot, some mugs, and tea. This was a lesson in enjoying a morning.

Jayne eventually dropped us near the trail, which lay just across a railroad tracks. She had to take us in two batches. I left in the first group, along with Scalpel and Moose. When the second carload arrived, we compared pack weights. Peru hoisted Moose's. "What do you have in there?" His bag got passed around, everyone expressing amazement at the heft. When finally it came back to Moose he lifted it with a puzzled expression.

"Why is this so heavy?" Moose is a solid hunk of a man, so I was relieved to know that even he thought this pack too weighty. As he set it down again, a clanking sound rang out. Those in on the joke burst out laughing. Moose reached in and one at a time pulled out 10 railroad spikes Scalpel had surreptitiously slipped inside. Some people have a gift of practical humor and Scalpel is one such. Whenever I try stuff like that, people just think I'm a jerk, but he pulls it off.

Our slackpacking brought us northward to the Three Sisters Wilderness, named after three gorgeous volcanoes. The trail winds past each in turn. We tackled them in a single, stunning, 30-mile day.

I hadn't particularly looked forward to the Three Sisters because I had been there (on a different route) once before, in 2001. On that trip, a steady rain obscured views and caused me to lose the trail. I mostly remembered it as a gray, boring place. But the gorgeous weather rendered it an entirely different scene now. The lupines bloomed in such a state of effulgence that their perfume hung thickly in the air, their colors framing a perfect base for the majestic snowy peaks.

The first part of the day involved a dry hot stretch, with nothing but silty creeks. Streams fed by runoff from glaciers transport minerals that the glaciers have accumulated, often giving the water an unpleasant taste and feel. We didn't mind the lack of water since our loads were light and the views unspeakably fine, but the mid-afternoon sun had us eagerly looking forward to Obsidian Falls. Here Gourmet, Moose, and I all took a turn standing under the beating and brutally cold force of the falls. Knut snapped a photo of me emerging with a look of sheer joy on my face.

Minutes thereafter, I made a snow angel in a small snowfield. I love the incongruity of the snow's appearance on blistering afternoons. I skipped uncharacteristically ahead of the others, though most passed me again before it was all said and done. In the late afternoon, the terrain turned to red volcanic pumice—hell on the boots and the feet, but these weird, barren formations made for some of my favorite hiking. The trail wound its way up an improbably high lava field for an eerie and breathtaking view that allowed even an unimaginative person as myself to reconstruct the eruption.

All throughout Northern California, Oregon, and Washington, we traversed volcanic terrain. Usually, we trod where the eruptions had been many thousands of years previous, allowing enough time for at least a thin layer of soil to form. I loved walking across the more recent and bare fields of hardened lava. Occasionally a small plant or shrub would somehow take hold and imperceptibly break down the rock with its roots, only to enter its death thralls shortly thereafter. It would leave a miniscule amount of organic material to be used as food by the next seed unlucky enough to germinate there. Insects, too, left decaying carcasses in the wake of their lives. I liked to scan these miles of red rock and envision them thousands of years later, covered with enough soil to feed a diverse ecosystem.

As wonderful as it was to have a nearly weightless hike, I found myself eager to resume true backpacking by the end of the week. I enjoy being able to camp away from the roads, and to have the flexibility to change plans over the course of the day. Don't get me wrong, if I ever do another long distance hike I will definitely welcome another stretch of slackpacking here and there, but it did make me appreciate true backpacking all the more.

While I was ready to be done with slackpacking, I was sorry to say goodbye to my new friends from Team All Dead. Knut and I had to get to town to resupply, but the rest of the group were pushing ahead to a different resupply point.

We found the last room available in the town of Sisters, where we took a zero day. When we returned to the trail, I brought with me an unusual assortment of foods:

carrots, apples, cheese, spinach, roast beef, salami, and good heavy bread. I had reached my limit of backpacker food. The last few days I'd had to force myself to choke down my rations of peanut butter and crackers. I refused to take one more step sustained by what I had been eating for more than a thousand miles. The carrots pushed my pack weight into the realm of the ridiculous, and by the end of the five days before the next resupply the salami was rather ripe, but even half-rancid lunch meat beat out peanut butter in appeal.

We hiked up to Minto Pass, situated in an area heavily damaged by fire. I hated to pitch a tent in such places, not only because of the fear of a dead tree falling on me, but because of the disruption caused to the flora at a sensitive stage of regrowth. But almost magically, we came across one small, tent-sized grove of living evergreens. We tucked ourselves in.

The following day began with terrific views of Three-Fingered Jack, an odd craggy set of peaks. The rest of the day we had Mount Jefferson in our sights—a mountain any founding father could be proud to call his namesake. A series of three creeks lay ahead, all reputed to be difficult fords. Considering how easy the crossings had been up to this point, we weren't too concerned, but one never wants to get too cocky about such things. The first creek indeed proved quite passable. I don't believe we even removed our boots. The second one presented an interesting problem. At some point over the winter, an avalanche had sloughed vast quantities of snow from the mountain above onto the creek-bed. The densely packed snow still completely covered the water, which rushed down precipitous falls just downstream from the crossing. We could hear the water roaring underneath the snow, but not see it. This was a potentially dangerous situation. If the snow bridge were too thin, we could fall into the rushing creek, getting pulled under the snow where we might get stuck and drown, or we might not get stuck but rather get swept over the falls.

The snow appeared thick and sturdy. We made a study of the banks, but no other good option for crossing presented itself. Knut went first. I waited at the bank to avoid adding any weight to the snow, then I crossed as well. No problem.

The third ford was the measliest of all. In fact, we weren't even quite sure when we had crossed it, it was so small.

For the last few days, we had heard that the trail might be closed up ahead due to fires. Up until we left for Sisters, we hoped we might get through the area while it remained open. Then we heard that there was for sure a closure, but a small one that could be navigated with only about an extra 10 miles of walking. We camped just south of where the detour started. That night large spongy columns of smoke rested above an orange glow in the still air; their eerie beauty transfixed us.

The next morning we set out on the detour. I really have to hand it to the Forest Service personnel who traipsed out there to post detour signs for the sake of our safety. I mean, it's not like they didn't have a few other things going on.

The side trails gave us a renewed appreciation for the PCT, which is nearly always well maintained with a moderate grade. The detour followed a steep, rocky, narrow path that was at times difficult to find. It spilled us out onto a gravel road, where we found additional signage verifying the detour. Staying on the route, we plunged back into the woods, now a lovely lowland forest, before re-emerging at another road. To our dismay, the signage had changed. The fire closure had expanded. If we had been just half an hour earlier, we might have gotten down the path before they widened the closure area. As it was, the detour would now add at least 20 miles rather than 10. We reminded ourselves that we were getting off easy compared to some of the hikers behind us who had faced periodic fire closures as early as the 79th mile of the trek.

The route took us to a paved road, which seemed promising. We hoped I might catch a ride and take Knut's pack with me so he could walk his continuous footsteps without his heavy pack. We walked on and on until the sun started sinking low and we knew we had missed our window of opportunity for hitchhiking. Still we walked on, wanting to cover as much of the roadwalk as we could in the cool of the night rather than face it in the heat of the day.

Just as the sun was sinking, a passing truck stopped in the middle of the road. "You want a ride?" It was a Park Service employee off to check on the closure boundaries. "I have to post some signs up the way, but I'll be back by in a few and can give you a lift." Away she went.

Knut started going through his bag to find his small daypack, into which he put his flashlight, some food and water, his sleeping pad and his sleeping bag. The small bag already bulged when I suggested he take the ground cloth. He said he could manage a night without it. Before he could even finish getting organized, our trail angel's headlights came back in view. Everything was rushed, but we agreed to a rendezvous point. Off I went with Knut's pack as he set off by foot under a clear starry sky.

The ranger seemed pretty keyed up, as you might expect from someone working a long adrenaline-filled day. She said the fire had suddenly run four miles overnight, which was why they had to broaden the closure area. She asked me and another hiker she had picked up if we knew who was ahead of and behind us, as it was part of her job to make sure everyone was out of danger. We gave her the best information we could.

The other hiker said he'd heard that the fire had started on tribal land and asked if that was why it had run out of control. He said he heard that the tribes don't like to ask for help from the federal government. No, the ranger replied, he was misinformed: when there is a fire everyone pitches in. She obviously had a lot of respect for the tribal firefighters. I'm not sure where the other hiker had gotten his information or if it had perhaps come from some preformed idea he was already carrying.

A small line of light still lingered on the horizon when she dropped us off. The other hiker decided to carry on a bit farther—he was one of those fast-moving sorts that I knew I would never see again. I pitched my tent. After eating, I stayed outside to enjoy the cool mosquito-free night. A screechy bird call, almost like an eagle, caught my attention. Looking around, I noticed several large birds, apparently owls. With great swooping silent wings they slowly arced over my tent and flew toward the rising crescent moon. I've always wondered what kind of owl would hunt in a group like that, or could they have been migrating? It was now August 20, perhaps some do start to migrate that early. I later asked a volunteer at an Audubon center about it and she was as puzzled as I was. I have used the Cornell Ornithology Lab's excellent online resource to try to identify the screeching call I heard, and I think it could well have been made by a female great horned owl. (I am using the word "screech" here to describe a sound like a rusty hinge, and not a sound like that made by the little screech owl.) But I am still not so sure about the fact that there were so many of them. Their mystery infused the night with still more beauty.

What a way to spend time alone in the mountains. Though I loved sharing the experience of the trail with Knut, I sometimes still missed having my own campsite. Tonight provided the best of both worlds, with me enjoying the solitude of a gorgeous evening, knowing that tomorrow I would reconnect with my hiking partner.

At 2 a.m. rain drops began to fall. I allowed the droplets to fall on my face for some time, unable to believe that after four months and 2,000 miles with no rain, the one night Knut was out there with no rain gear was the night the heavens sent rain. He hadn't even taken the ground cloth! When the rain increased, I guiltily attached my rain fly.

The next morning I dried out the fly, ate a leisurely breakfast, and rearranged my pack a bit. I left a note for Knut and carried both our packs the 0.8 mile to the trail to try to find a campsite since I expected him to take all day reaching me. I had just settled in to the shade to catch up on my journal when to my surprise Knut came along! He had managed the rain pretty well and laughed about his rotten luck. He had also made a short cut where the road made a bend, cutting his mileage.

The next day brought us our first views of Mount Hood, dear to me not only because of its beauty but because of its proximity to the city of Portland, where I've spent happy vacations visiting Scott and other friends. Many's the time I've considered relocating to Portland, though I can never quite make the leap

TOILET PAPER IN OREGON

I don't quite know why, but the Oregon backcountry seems to draw people who are incapable of even attempting to bury their toilet paper. In places, it wandered around like stained tumbleweed. My theory is that Oregon draws a greater portion of its population from people raised in other states than do California or Washington. People not reared in the backcountry ethic come to Oregon and suddenly get the wilderness bug. They proceed without having gotten the memo about how to dispose of their waste and somehow imagine the toilet paper will just sort of disappear after a day or two. I have no idea if any portion of my theory holds a bit of water, but I won't let facts get in the way of my pronouncement!

***

to leave winter behind. Portlanders like to remind me that if I want snow I can drive up into the mountains any time I like. I like to remind them that they are a bunch of pampered sissies.

In the morning I set off by myself as usual. While Knut finished his granola breakfast at camp, I munched on granola bars as I marched along. I had just tucked the fourth and final wrapper into my pocket when a wing-shaped shadow brushed my face. I looked up in time to see a long-eared owl come to light on a branch. As soon as it stood still, the owl became virtually invisible. Only by counting branches could I relocate the bird once I looked away and back again.

The owl and I stood watching each other a long time. In the midst of this peaceful moment came the familiar call of the bowels. Giving the owl an apologetic farewell wave, I headed off the trail to find a suitable place. I dug my hole, squatted and did my thing. While I was in the inglorious act of wiping, a shadow once again swept across my face. I looked up to see the owl perched more closely than before, her wise old face letting me know just how ridiculous I looked with my pants around my ankles and a piece of toilet paper in my hand. I often felt humbled by nature on my hike, but this time I felt downright humiliated.

The effect soon wore off and my mind returned to how I might refill the contents of my stomach. Mount Hood is home to Timberline Lodge, which in turn is home to an all-you-can-eat buffet. The cost of the buffet is not insignificant ($20), so for once in my greedy life I had been planning on passing it up. But with it now less than a day's hike away, I felt willpower slipping away.

To me, this was all Timberline Lodge represented: a potential food source. I'm sure other more civilized hikers had discussed its charms, but my stomach must have turned a deaf ear. All for the better, since my ignorance allowed me to enjoy one of the nicest surprises made by human hands on the PCT.

Perched at nearly 6,000 feet, Timberline couldn't be more picturesque. If you have seen the movie "The Shining" you have seen the exterior of the building already, as it plays the part of the Overlook Hotel. The ascent to the lodge granted us frequent views of Mount Adams to the south as we clambered over the occasional snowfield dotted with hawthorn bushes. Hood's peak loomed magnificently and immediately to the north. Typically, I find myself annoyed when human-made structures are inserted into such scenic locations, but not this time.

First, I got caught up in Knutella's enthusiasm for the Norwegian banner that fluttered in the row of flags out front. He pulled out his camera and attempted to snap a photo that would capture the Norwegian colors in all their glory without any contamination from the Swedish flag next to it. To the uninitiated, Scandinavian flags all look alike. Each bears the same-shaped cross and the trick is to remember which country has which colors. The Finnish flag is a simple blue cross on a white background. The Danish is a white cross on a red background. The Swedes boast a yellow cross on a blue background. Both the Icelandic and Norwegian people seem to think a little much of themselves as they feel entitled to three colors on their flags. The Icelandic flag has a red cross with a white lining on a blue background, whereas the apparently more thrilling Norwegian flag has a blue cross with a white lining on a red background. Still more cross variations arise if you start to look at the symbols for places like the Faroe Islands, Shetland Islands, Orkney Islands, and others around Scandinavia. So when Knut attempted to crop out Sweden, I pretended to know which flag was getting the boot and cheered him on.

Once my companion satisfied his national pride, we entered the lodge where some of the world's finest rustic-style artwork greeted us. Various Depression-era artists had hand-carved nearly everything in this George Stanley Underwood building, which was underwritten in part by the Works Progress Administration. Every detail in the stonework, the woodwork, the windows, and other details spoke of the pride the craftspeople took in building this structure 70 years ago. Although the lodge is now operated privately rather than by the government, the operators have done a wonderful job of maintaining that sense of public spirit. Nothing is over-commercialized or tacky. I hope to come back to this building at some point to appreciate its museum-quality artwork more fully (and to visit their actual museum on the lower level).

As it was, my stomach urged me to check out the lunch situation. Fortune smiled on us, for the buffet was set to start at 11, and we arrived just a few minutes before. Frankly, we would have been thrilled with pretty much any food so long as it arrived in quantity, but we were blown away by the quality of this luncheon. Cheeses and meats whose names I couldn't pronounce, fresh fruit, lightly steamed vegetables, dark crusty breads, fluffy pastry desserts, then back again to the cheese, meat, and fruits. I am certain the establishment lost money by the time we finally threw in the napkin around 1:30.

We staggered out of the dining hall and toppled onto some chairs in the lobby. We looked at each other with uncomprehending eyes: how could something so wonderful disable us so completely? We had planned to resume hiking in the early afternoon, but after that feast all we could do was to sit there nodding off uncomfortably. Eventually, along about 5 we waddled away from the lodge to continue our northward way.

The following day rewarded our dedication with the first glimpses of Mount St. Helens and Mount Rainier. Like Palin's Russia, Washington was within our sights! Hood and Adams continued to grace our southward view. On days like this we easily remembered why we lugged 40-pound packs up and down mountains all day.

As much as these mountains filled me with joy, one thing instilled even more happiness in my heart—Scott was coming to meet us at the small town of Cascade Locks on the Oregon/Washington border! When I had called him from Timberline Lodge and harangued him into making the trip out from his Portland home, I let him know we would be there no later than 5 on Saturday, August 25.

Knutella and I decided to take the reputedly spectacular alternate Eagle Creek Trail to Cascade Locks. We camped Friday night at Indian Springs campground, where the PCT and the alternate intersect. As we were making dinner, a southbound hiker hoisted herself up from the steep Eagle Falls route and planted herself at the intersection as well. Knut and I were always happy to see other hikers, but she was downright

THE WORKS PROGRESS ADMINISTRATION

Toward the end of the Great Depression, President Roosevelt championed nearly $11 billion in federal spending to put nine million people to work and build up the infrastructure. From 1935 to1943, craftsmen and laborers built more than half a million miles of roads, and tens of thousands of bridges and public buildings, as well as thousands of parks and other public spaces such as airports.

In one of the sub-programs, artists were employed for a variety of projects in the public interest. Writers wrote tour guides, actors and orchestras traveled to rural areas that rarely had access to top-notch entertainment, and visual artists contributed to projects such as the Timberline Lodge, as well as more modest works such as murals you may still find on your hometown post office.

***

ecstatic. This talented Canadian had come all the way across Washington and in the 30 days since she set out, this was the first night she wasn't camping alone.

Southbounders are a special breed. While hundreds of us set out heading north every year, fewer than 20 start in Canada and head south. The reasons for this are many. First, snow often prevents them from starting until late July or early August. Second, the late start means that they have to be in good enough shape to make long miles coming right out of the chute or they won't get across the Sierras before the snowstorms make that range impassable. Third, by the time they get to Southern California, what little water northbounders enjoyed will largely be dried up. Yet a southbound hike appeals to one's sense of ruggedness, and to the desire to be mostly alone in the wilderness. I have often thought that if I ever try the Continental Divide Trail I would be tempted to start at the north.

We tried not to bother every southbounder we saw (though they numbered less than 10 by our reckoning), knowing they had to run a gauntlet of northbounders for hundreds of miles. But sometimes we would strike up a conversation. On one such occasion we encountered two men hiking together, one a Canadian and the other Slovakian. When the latter told me where he was from, his utterly American accent confused me. I thought perhaps that, just as there is an Athens, Georgia, and a Paris, Texas, perhaps there was a place called Slovakia, Oregon. So I began to ask a clarifying question but got no farther than, "When you say Slovakia ..." before Knut, as if teaching simple math to a child, explained, "It's a country in Europe." My geography is as famously bad as any American's, but I did know that much! (Granted, I would not have been able to locate Slovakia on a map.)

After camping at Indian Springs, we managed to break camp fairly early for once and began to cover the roughly 15 miles down to Cascade Locks. The steep initial descent offered a fun, if brief, change of pace from the accommodating standards of the PCT. We shortly found ourselves winding along rocky bluffs above Eagle Creek, thoroughly enjoying the serenity and unique views afforded by our miniature canyon. As more and more tributaries flowed into the creek and as the creek hurled itself toward the Colombia, we were treated to a few extraordinary cascades. The king of these cascades sends water 160 feet straight down at Tunnel Falls. Trail builders carved a narrow path into the basalt walls of the canyon, providing a thrilling approach. Upon reaching the falls, the trail tucks itself behind them, into a brief tunnel that soon pops out the other side. In spite of the deafening roar, the place felt to me like the inner sanctum of a church. I lingered to savor a specialness I don't usually find at the hands of human alterations.

All morning we had been meeting a few people with packs coming up to the mountains for some R&R. At first we didn't mind this steady trickle of weekenders. Fridays, Saturdays, and Sundays nearly always brought us into contact with the more civilized classes and typically we enjoyed chatting with them. Often these were locals who might tell us something interesting about the flora, fauna, or geology. Sometimes they would even give us food.

But shortly after passing the falls, the trail traffic really picked up. Now it wasn't just backpackers but day-hikers. Usually we were perfectly happy to see day-hikers too, but we weren't accustomed to seeing them in this volume. As the morning wore on and we came nearer the trailhead, the path became downright clogged. And I realize this is going to sound ridiculous coming from someone who by this time had a colossal stench emitting from every pore of her body and every fiber of clothing, but a lot of these people *stank*. I have never been fond of perfumed body products, but over the course of the hike I had become extremely sensitive to them. I could smell each drop of aftershave, hair-spray, deodorant, cologne, laundry detergent and hand lotion to such a degree that at times it knocked the breath out of me. Knut and I practically held our noses as we navigated the throng.

By the time we reached the parking lot near the town, we were pretty much clawing our way past the locals. And by this point, it wasn't just a matter of wanting a little solitude for spiritual reasons, there were more serious issues at stake. As soon as we emerged onto asphalt we accosted the first passer-by to find out where the nearest latrine was located. We marched double time with tightened buttocks to the sturdy-looking shithouse on a small hill. A piece of paper under a rock caught my eye as I made my way—a note from Memphis Tim for Knutella and me!

Memphis picked berries prolifically, and I always joked that you never wanted to be hiking behind Memphis in a berry patch because you would be left with nothing. But here he had found a huge mess of blackberries that exceeded even his appetite. In his kindness, he left a note to let us know where to find them—near the aforementioned shithouse.

After taking care of business, I phoned Scott from the parking lot. "Hey Scott, just to let you know, we'll be in Cascade Locks about 2, but no rush."

"2? I thought you said it would be 5."

"Well, two days ago I wasn't sure exactly when we'd arrive."

"I can't get there by 2."

"Yeah, no worries. We've got plenty to do. Whenever you get here, it will be great to see you." Scott doesn't always like a change in plans unless he is the one doing the changing. The best thing is to speak slowly and soothingly until he recognizes that the new situation poses no threat. There was a short pause.

"How will I find you?"

"I've got my cell phone. I'll give a call to let you know where we are."

"Well, I've got a lot to get done today. I don't know when I'll get there."

Frankly, after my terrible treatment of him the last time I saw him, I was relieved to recover the moral high ground through his crankiness. But actually I knew him well enough to know he wasn't truly cranky, he just wanted to make sure I knew he hadn't flaked out about my arrival time. "Sure, no problem," I assured him. "We'll just be relaxing, no hurry."

Pause.

"Okay Gailie Mae. Can't wait to see you." Whew. When he calls me Gailie Mae (which isn't actually my name) I know we are on solid ground.

Our boots now tread almost at sea level. In fact, once we got to Cascade Locks just down the highway, we would be at 116 feet—the lowest point on the PCT. We found a shady spot on the mown grass to have first lunch and to adjust to the volume of humans. Normally, we wouldn't have had to sit around looking pathetic very long before someone would offer us a ride, but the day was still young and there wasn't much outgoing traffic, so we eventually shouldered our packs and walked the final easy miles into town.

Upon arrival, Knut and I secured a hotel room, then ventured out for food. We ensconced ourselves into a booth at the local diner and were soon joined by the Brits and Running Wolf. We had second lunch (or possibly first supper) while awaiting Scott's arrival.

I was just licking my chops as I finished second supper when I saw him approaching the restaurant. I tried to hop up and run to the door in greeting, but by this time my feet didn't like sudden movements. They cramped up when making almost any motion other than hiking—a condition that lasted for months after I completed the PCT. I did hop up, then sort of tottered sideways. I more or less straightened out and kind of sidled across the floor. I had mostly regained my composure by the time he opened the door to give me one of his trademark whirl-in-the-air hugs. "You're light as a feather!" Scott always says such things no matter how heavy I actually am.

"You're strong as an ox!" I declared when he set me back down. This is actually true.

I introduced him around and ordered him a beer. The first of many we would have that evening. After a bit, the Brits and other hikers who had come around begged off to join a party someone was throwing for hikers in a nearby park. After another round, Knut decided he felt like hitting the sack. So Scott and I bought a six-pack or two and carried them over to the party. I commented as we made our way across the uneven terrain that I should have brought my headlamp since it would be dark by the time we walked back. Scott scoffed at this, claiming he had exceptional night vision and wouldn't need artificial light.

I didn't find the Brits or many other hikers I knew at the party, so Scott and I settled into a grassy spot on the bank of the Columbia a bit removed from the noise. We talked about old friends, familiar fears, and eternal hopes. It seems for the last 20 years we have been finding new ways to have the same conversations.

When we finally decided to stand up and head back, the half-moon had already set, leaving the night pitch black. I again complained about forgetting my head lamp but Scott strode boldly ahead, crowing once more about his excellent night vision. "It must be something unique about my ocular physiology, because my eyesight right now is remarkably—" He got no further because he toppled head first over an enormous knee-high boulder. The beer bottles flew out of his hands, which were now splayed next to his head on the ground. I was glad I couldn't see properly because I was sure he had mangled his legs or developed a head wound and that would have been too much to bear. But then I heard his gruff laughter. "As I was saying," he continued, "I can see perfectly ..."

I cackled and went to check on the beer.

The next morning, Knutella and I took ruthless advantage of my friend, having him drive us to the next town since the store at Cascade Locks offered very little in the way of hiking food. We also bought extra food to ship ahead to Stehekin in northern Washington. Since it was Sunday, we foisted the job of mailing the food on Scott as well. Then he took us to a coffee shop where we checked email. I hope that whoever is reading this will believe that in real life I am not really such a moocher, but by now I had become pretty shameless in my eagerness to achieve Canada.

When Scott dropped us off back at Cascade Locks, we said our farewells, but not for long. We would see him again in about a month, once we completed the trail. Feeling lucky and uplifted, we eagerly launched into our final 500 miles.

WASHINGTON

The PCT crosses into Washington on the wonderful-ly-named Bridge of the Gods. This modern structure of steel takes its name from a natural land bridge which had dammed the Columbia for decades after a landslide some centuries past. Our knowledge of this comes to us from Native American historians; while geologists of diverse backgrounds continue to work to understand more about the exact dates and mechanism of the former dam.

The crossing of the modern structure did not provide the exhilarating experience it might have. The narrow, busy bridge has no walkway, so I hugged the side rails. I would have loved to have stood in the middle of the bridge to savor the moment of crossing state lines, but instead I hustled myself into the Evergreen State.

As I entered Washington, part of me felt that making it the rest of the way was now a sure thing, and part of me remembered all the stories of people who got within miles of the border only to break their ankle or suffer similar misfortune. Still, only 500 miles now stood between me and Canada. When I had hiked my first 500 miles down in Southern California, I felt like I had made such a major accomplishment. Now I was like, "500 miles? Meh, no biggie."

Of course, I knew that the relative ease or challenge of this final stretch would all depend on the weather. We crossed into Washington on August 26. September is typically at first rainy and then snowy up in the mountains that lay ahead.

Moreover, the territory is some of the most remote and rugged in the lower 48 states. In good weather, the backcountry of Washington's Cascade Range is without exaggeration one of the most spectacular places in the world. In bad weather it is not only treacherous, but the occluded views are of limited interest.

Several years earlier, I had taken a five-day trip in Washington's North Cascades National Park. After three of the most gorgeous days of August weather and crystal clear views, a cold front moved in. Rain came down in an undramatic but thoroughly drenching and relentless stream. The rivers swelled, creating difficult fords. During the brief periods when the rain subsided, the dense brush at the side of the trail still held enough moisture to continue to drench me and my companion. I hadn't brought rain pants and my rain jacket did not hold up. Within a few hours, I started coming down with early stages of hypothermia. We stopped and set up the tent, trying to get me warmed up, but met with limited success. We made the decision to leave the heaviest of our wet gear and march out the final 15 miles as fast as possible. The trail had been freshly swept away in some spots, in other spots the rain had sloughed the earth from higher up and deposited it on our path. We made it out, but when we wanted to go back to retrieve our gear a few days later, we had to get special dispensation from the Park Service because they had closed the trail due to all the damage the rain had done.

This memory had been weighing on my mind ever since leaving the Mexican border. I vividly remembered how dicey things would have been if I had been alone in that earlier situation, so Knut's company gave me added reasons for gratitude as we entered this state where things could go either way.

We soon began seeing one of the first sure signs that summer was passing to fall—wooly caterpillars. I wished I had learned the ancient art of predicting how hard the winter would be by the appearance of the stripes on their bodies. It's not so much that I believe in that sort of divination, but rather at this point I was always on the lookout for some new way to pass the time and take my mind off the various aches and pains I had acquired. The worst of which was an increasing pain in my feet.

In Southern California I had big problems with blisters and—especially in the beginning—with bruised soles. Periodically some problem or another had cropped up with my feet since then, but overall they hadn't caused me as much difficulty as I had assumed they would. Now a great deal of cramping afflicted my foot muscles, especially when I first started walking or if I stood still for long, and other pains felt like renewed bruising but were possibly plantar fasciitis. My arches—never ones to stay as upright as I might like in the first place—were becoming reluctant to rise to the occasion at all. I found that I could control the worst of the pain associated with these problems by taking a few ibuprofens a day, so I was much luckier than many who really struggled with terrible pain. Yet by the time we crossed this last state border, nearly every hiker knew that only a major accident would keep him or her from completing the trek. One could see determined people working their way down the path in all sorts of contorted positions without a word of complaint.

An August 28 journal entry illustrates my own contented state of mind that first night in Washington. "The day ended with a walk along some lava fields, I always love that. Now we are at a campground with picnic tables and a latrine. Feeling spoiled."

The following day marked the last time we worried over water, and it was due to an uncharacteristic lack of vigilance in which we misidentified a lake, believing it to be the penultimate rather than ultimate water source for a dozen or so miles. Fortunately, the fairly mild weather made it easy to make do with about a half liter each. We even felt a bit smug that our packs were a few pounds lighter than they would have been if we had been on the ball. The occasional berry-gorging undoubtedly helped us stay hydrated.

When we neared roads through public lands, however, we were often out-competed by local berry-pickers enjoying a healthy method of supplementing the stores in their larders. Some pickers also harvest the wild berries commercially, in accordance with certain laws and restrictions. On this day we came across a family from the Warm Springs Indian Reservation, which the PCT had crossed way down in Oregon. These three pickers (a little girl, her mother, and grandmother) explained that for some reason the berries on their land hardly produced a thing this year, so they were having to venture rather far afield for their berries. We chatted with them a bit. The little girl scarcely said a word but I could see her mind working when the mother explained to her how that one trail where they live stretches all the way down to Mexico and up to Canada and that we had walked the whole way. I always wonder how children too young to grasp maps and distances envision this sort of trek.

I had now come roughly 2,200 miles without having to face my dread fear of wild dogs. But on the second-to-last morning of August, I set out by myself as usual. While I stopped for my bowel movement, Knut got ahead of me. I had resumed the solitary wooded trail when I heard dogs. Their barks made them sound large and angry. I pulled out the map to confirm what I knew: there were no settlements nearby. These dogs were making their way in life by attacking and killing other animals. Just think how happy they would be if they could stumble upon an animal not only tasty in her own right but also silly enough to be carrying several days' worth of food!

"They aren't going to attack me. They aren't going to attack me." I repeated the words like a mantra, and it did seem to ward them off at first. Their snarls receded for a time and

I relaxed my pace again. As long as there were no wild dogs around, I wanted to enjoy my morning's solitude. But when their barking again edged closer I suddenly recalled all my fond feelings for Knut and how much I would enjoy his company. I hustled down the trail.

The animals were terrifyingly close by the time I caught sight of Knut's large black pack resting against a log, and my suntanned friend reclining next to it as if he were not about to ripped apart by savage beasts. Knut faced away from me, looking down a ravine. When I came closer he heard my footfalls and turned to greet me. His face shone and I thought he was about to announce that he had slain the devil dogs.

"I saw a great stag!" he announced.

My mind reeled. Great stag … great stag … . "Oh, you saw a bull elk!"

"Yes!"

"But what about the dogs, did you hear the wild dogs?" I blurted this out before I could remember that a bull elk (and frankly "great stag" sounds way cooler) is actually a gorgeous sight to behold. One worthy of taking a little time for marveling over the experience with one's significant other. Knut knew all about my unreasonable fear, however and I watched the stag-induced wonder drain from his face as he assured me that although he had seen the two large dogs that were barking so aggressively, they had not tried to approach.

"They went that way," he pointed down the ravine.

"Whew!" I sat down on the log next to him and quite bravely decided not to ask him more detailed questions about the dogs even though his answers might lead to additional clues as to whether they would be inclined to stalk and attack at the hour of their choosing. Incredibly, we did not have any additional trouble with the canines.

We carried our packs into the stunning Mount Adams Wilderness, where melting glaciers provided perfect habitat for the mosquitoes. The plague of insects made it difficult to enjoy the terrific views for much of the day, though from one windy ridge we were able to pause to take in the panoramic sight of three volcanoes—Adams, Rainier, and St. Helens.

The water up in glacier country is usually not delicious since it carries mineral-heavy silt, so we enthusiastically awaited a spring near the end of a lava field where the trail started to lose elevation again. According to some, Lava Spring provided the best water on the entire PCT. By this time, I was a water connoisseur and glacier runoff ranked lower than pasture creeks in flavor. At the other end of the spectrum, springs often put out water so utterly delicious that only a sommelier's vocabulary could do it justice.

I intentionally passed over some very nice water sources, wanting to fill all my containers at Lava Spring. Imagine my disappointment when the flavor was no better than other silt-laden water typical to the area. Nonetheless, the stop was not a total waste, since it was here we met Red, a section hiker we would meet off and on for the rest of the trip. She had thru-hiked a couple years earlier and now was re-hiking Washington. She had two very cool tattoos, one on each forearm. On the right were the Korean characters for her family's name on her mother's side. On the left was the Scottish coat-of-arms for her family on her father's side. If I were to do something similar I would mostly just have two armfuls of German imagery, which would frankly be kind of creepy.

That evening an examination of our food bags and our maps caused us to plan to push out 27 miles the next day to reach the resupply box waiting for us in the small community of White Pass.

I am happy to say that our plans did not come to fruition. Instead, we hiked a mere 16 miles the next day through Goat Rocks Wilderness. Whenever anyone asks Knut or me what was the best thing we saw on the trail, we give an answer like, "Well, there were so many great things that I can't pick just one thing, but it would be hard to beat the Goat Rocks Wilderness."

The trail through the Wilderness area begins with a breathtaking lupine-studded ascent that never lets a hiker's eyes rest from the beauty of Mount Rainier, Mount St. Helens, and Mount Adams, all looming over high alpine meadows. After a few hours we came up to a pass near the peak of Old Snowy Mountain. Here, our pleasure at the breathtaking view was marred only by two adolescent boys who kept hurling large rocks off the pass. The reasons for our displeasure at this activity were as follows:

It was loud and annoying.

We felt it was not unlikely that the rocks being hurled from this distance could easily land on unseen hikers, skiers, or climbers on the snow below.

Even if the rocks did not strike people, they still might strike animals like the mountain goat we did see on a snowy shelf roughly in the line of fire.

Even if no humans or other animals were struck directly, the activity could cause an avalanche, endangering all below.

We loudly discussed these possibilities within earshot of the man who seemed to be their father. He told the boys to knock it off and said they had to leave now. Since he had been saying that exact thing for at least half an hour already, the boys of course paid no heed. If anything, the rate of boulder-hurling accelerated. Knut went so far as to say something directly to the man—a rare occasion for my stoic Norwegian friend. The man replied with a helpless look and more ineffectual yelling at the boys.

We moved away from the family to enjoy a break farther up the pass where the trail divides into the hiker route and the stock route. We had decided the previous night to take the stock route because it would save us time—we were planning a high-mileage day after all. Red had told us that both routes were terrifying: the hiker route ascended an exposed narrow trail with steep drop-offs on either side while the stock route conveyed hikers across an exposed narrow trail covered in ice with a steep drop-off on only one side. However, earlier in the day we met some southbound hikers who told us that the stock route had a 30-foot stretch of ice that would prevent life-loving hikers from going that route, whereas the hiker route was clear. We hadn't made up our minds yet as to which way to go, deciding to wait until we could see things for ourselves.

Now we looked both ways. From where we sat, the stock route did seem a bit dicey. The two worst spots were a rather small stretch at the beginning—about 10 feet long—and then later another 30-foot stretch. Still, it seemed manageable, so we went for it. The going was slow and one didn't want to look down too much, but all was well until we reached the 30-foot ice-covered segment. From a distance, it had looked more snowy than icy, but now that we were up on it, we could see it for the solid ice it was. We kicked it to determine whether it was soft enough to let us make steps, but the sun had only just started shining on it, so it was still rock hard. We decided to eat our lunch there and see if another hour of sunshine would soften it up enough to give us a better passage.

No sooner had we pulled out our food bags than rocks started falling on us from the hiker trail above. Suddenly it didn't seem like such a good lunch spot. We hemmed and hawed, reluctant to go forward and reluctant to turn back. We both felt that there was at least a 95 percent chance of making it across with no problem, but if one of us did slip it would be curtains for that person. We reluctantly decided the best thing was to turn around. As we headed back to the trail junction, an older woman approached us saying she had found the hiker route so unpleasant that she had changed her mind and would now try the stock route. She had a nice light pack that kept her nimble, and she probably had better

balance than we did in general. When she got to the dangerous part, she surveyed it for some time before deciding to
give it a go. She made it across without a problem, fortunately, but we could hardly bear to watch.

When we returned to where the trail divided, we were
met by a hiker we barely knew, who more or less called us
sissies for not continuing on the stock route (though he too
opted for the hiker route, where we quickly left him behind).
His attitude did not impress me and was not characteristic
for long distance hikers. Most wilderness enthusiasts en-
courage fellow hikers to do no more than they feel safe doing, and rarely does anyone try to make anyone feel they
have something to prove.

As it turned out, we couldn't have been happier with our
choice. The hiker route carried us right up Old Snowy Mountain. We wouldn't have thought it possible to have views
surpassing what we had already seen that day, but the extra
elevation and the narrow terrain must have heightened our
senses, making everything around us even more thrilling.

In places the trail not only fell away steeply on either
side, but seemed to be falling away on the path ahead as
well! Patience and a refusal to give in to vertigo taxed my
mental stamina wonderfully, especially on the descent back
down to where the hiker route rejoined the stock route. But
then the fun was just beginning! The trail clung for miles to
the narrow spine of the mountain as we eyed the glaciers
immediately below us while the volcanic peaks still showed
off in the near distance.

When we finally found a spot wide enough for a rest,
we began asking each other why this place wasn't regularly
listed and discussed as one of the ultimate highlights of a
thru-hike. The only reason I could come up with was that
Washington's weather is so fickle. We were doing this stretch
on a sunny, clear day with only a slight breeze. I would not
have wanted to have been out there in the rain, the lighten-

ing, the snow, or the wind—any of which a typical hiker in a typical year could expect to encounter in the Goat Rocks. Indeed, I later met a man who had nearly thru-hiked the year before. Recall that the previous year had been extremely difficult, with heavy snow starting in the Sierras and carrying right through into Washington. To get as far as Goat Rocks in 2011, a hiker had to be pretty darn tough. This man had made it all that way and then found himself crawling on his hands and knees through the snow in high winds to get past the stretch we now found so wonderful. After that, with less than 400 miles to go, he quit the trail.

Even in the good weather we experienced, the trail wiped us out after only 16 miles. We called it a day—and a mighty fine one at that! The next morning the views just kept coming, especially of cloud-wreathed Mount Rainier. Then as we descended toward White Pass, I proposed a shortcut along an old ski-lift trail to a gravel road. Knut, having a keen awareness of my navigational limitations, resisted at first but went along with it in the end. Incredibly enough, my shortcut worked out. This is possibly the only instance of navigation in which I was right and Knut was wrong. (Astute readers will note that I have not described very many instances of navigational disputes and will surmise that is because nearly every other anecdote would demonstrate my incompetence, or—nearly as bad—Knut's skill.)

We came into the small gas station/restaurant/grocery store in town to resupply—a depot called The Kracker Barrel. It was the one spot where I hadn't told anyone that I intended to pick up mail because I had it confused with The Cracker Barrel—that chain of restaurants which for years fired employees if they believed the worker was gay, lesbian, bisexual, or transgender. I didn't want anyone to know I would be slinking in there to pick up a package. Happily, this turned out to be a locally owned spot with terrific service. (And Cracker Barrel amended its policy a few years ago so that on paper at least they no longer discriminate against the queer community in their hiring practices.) We stayed the better part of the day, keeping company with Red, Running Wolf, and the Brits before heading back out on the trail.

The trail became crowded with weekenders as we were close to a road and it was Labor Day weekend, but we still found a pleasant and solitary spot to pitch a tent. After a relatively warm night we hadn't expected to go only a few hundred yards the next morning before encountering heavy frost still on the ground. More and more, nature reminded us that our hike would not last forever. The shorter days, the colder temperatures, the changing quality of the vegetation, all imparted feelings of both accomplishment and nostalgia.

Another indication of the changing season started up now too: elk hunters joined us in the mountains. Hunting seems to be a bellwether of culture in this country. Although I am mostly a vegetarian when I'm not hiking, I've never had any problem with responsible hunters. There are dozens of excellent reasons to hunt for your food, and there are hundreds of reasons to avoid factory-farmed meat. Unfortunately, a few hunters drink too much or otherwise disregard safety while hunting, but such folks usually only come out during the main rifle season for deer. In my experience, hunters who are serious enough to go in for bows, muzzleloaders, or who have waited for years to get their permits for elk or high bucks tend to be good folks.

Still, it's understandable that some people who have lived their lives away from hunting culture can't help but feel a little nervous when encountering heavily-weaponed and camouflaged men coming at them in the middle of the wilderness. (For some reason, all the elk hunters I encountered were in fact men.) Frankly, that nervousness probably demonstrates more common sense than my utter lack of concern at the same sight.

In fact, I don't recall just where this happened, but a few weeks earlier Knut had been walking alone and came behind another man, who suddenly turned to face my friend. To Knut's surprise, the man was pointing a custom-built rifle at him! The man let him on by. Not long thereafter, Knut caught up with me and told me what happened. I thought that, since Knut might not be used to seeing recreational gun users, he had perhaps misinterpreted events. But soon enough, the man came along and he didn't look friendly. He was dressed in camouflage accoutered with rows of ammo. On top of that I couldn't think what would be in season just then. "What are you hunting?" I called out cheerfully, trying to prove to Knut that it's only in the movies that Americans wander around in the woods being dangerous. "Nothin'," the man grunted in reply and kept striding. It's the sort of thing that does make a person think we might do better to have fewer guns out there.

During elk season and the high buck season that followed it, the hunters would ask if we had seen their quarry (we never had), and then about once a day we would run into wardens who would ask us if we had seen their quarry—hunters. Of course, they were only checking to make sure everyone was hunting lawfully and not hoping for wall trophies.

We now closed in on Snoqualmie Pass, where the trail intersects I-90. A gas station there holds packages for hikers, and I had a resupply box waiting for me. It was one of the last of the boxes that I had sent from home. Even though the fact that I had given up my stove meant these boxes no longer held that much for me, I still looked forward to whatever treats I had packed in there, and I enjoyed throwing some variety in the hiker boxes for those coming behind.

But before landing in Snoqualmie, Knut and I had a wallop of a falling out. It had started with me getting my nose out of joint at an insensitive comment, and then as fights have a habit of doing, snowballed in ways that made no sense and that are not worthy of reproducing here. The end result was that we made separate camps that night and by the time I set out in the morning Knut had already packed far down the trail.

Very often since Knut and I started hiking together, I had missed being able to go at my own pace, set my own breaks, and just generally not have to worry about anyone else's emotional status. Still, there was no doubt that my hiking experience had greatly improved since joining up with him. If Knut's intention were to outpace me, he'd have no problem doing so and in that case I would simply never see him again. He would just go back to Norway without another thought. I was too angry to miss him, but, although only 250 miles remained on the trek, old fears resurfaced. What if I were caught in a snowstorm? What if I fell and hurt myself? But most importantly of all, who would share the rest of the hike with me? With Knut, every wildlife sighting, every gorgeous sunset, every breathtaking panorama, and every startling flower lived in another heart besides my own. As a rather solitary person, I found myself deeply surprised by how much this turned out to matter to me. But even that wasn't the main thing on my mind just then.

I knew that eventually I would miss Knut's wry smile, his singing, his assortment of facts about the natural world, and his inexplicable tolerance of my bad jokes. But what upset me most of all right then was that Knut had left me carrying a heavy two-person tent all on my own. He had dumped it in my campsite the night before. Knut would probably just hitch into town to pick up a one-person tent to get him the rest of the way, while I lugged three extra pounds around. Jerk. For the first time in more than 1,000 miles, I cried. Pulled myself together. Cried some more.

Fortunately, I was in a "pulled myself together" stage when I heard a voice call out to me from the left. I saw Knut perched on a large flat boulder, waiting for me. I threw down my pack and we made up as senselessly as we had quarreled.

It was a good thing we had lifted our spirits by mending our feud since nothing about Snoqualmie Pass cheered our hearts to any degree. The gas station which was kind enough to hold packages did not make it easy. The owners tossed everything haphazardly into an old walk-in cooler that was deathly hot. Our poor friends the Brits never were able to locate their box there, and the food available for sale was of the lowest possible suitability for hikers. When I mailed an envelope from the privatized post office within the store, I had to explain to the clerk how to calculate the postage and even then she was uncertain enough that I paid extra just so she would have peace of mind. There was a hotel at the crossing as well, and our room lacked air conditioning (in spite of the frost a few days earlier, this day and night were stifling). In short, it was not the most pleasant stop, but it certainly wasn't a disaster either. We got what we needed and were even able to check email at the hotel.

I had hoped to meet my brother who lives in Seattle when I got to this point in the hike. Meanwhile Knut had hoped to meet his second cousin at this spot as well. We'd had a hard time coordinating these visits. We now had agreed to meet Knut's cousin at the next stop, about four days away. We really had to be there at the right time because she was flying all the way from Duluth in order to meet him. To make it we were going to have to get an early start the next morning, and with hiker midnight (roughly 8 p.m.) coming fast I had to send my regrets to my brother. We made plans to see each other after my trip wrapped up instead.

Now began a stunning and surprisingly quiet 70-mile stretch of trail. With easy access to highways on either end and unbelievable terrain, I would have expected it to be popular with local backpackers. Instead, once we got up onto the high alpine ridges, we hardly saw a soul. Well, that's not quite true, a large mountain goat kept ahead of us on the trail for a bit near sunset. These beautiful creatures (more closely related to antelopes than goats) have become a nuisance and worse in some parts of the Northwest where they have been transplanted, though they are native to the area I was then hiking.

When they overpopulate an area, these ruminants can become so eager for salt that they have been known to chase hikers who just urinated, hoping to get the human to produce still more for them to lick up. With their muscular builds and sturdy horns, they can be dangerous, one even killed a man in 2010.

My inclination was to enjoy the sight of such a beautiful creature and then keep moving, lest it follow and bother us. Knut, however, insisted on getting as close as possible and taking numerous photos. I have mixed emotions about the sort of person who wants to get good photos. I invariably feel annoyed and wish the person could just enjoy the moment, but later I am always asking for copies of the photos.

The sunlight was losing its warmth, but we calculated that we still had plenty of time to reach the next saddle where we would surely find a place to make camp. Marmots whistled and squeaked at us as we made our way. The path clung to the sheer mountains and I clung to the path, my vertigo barely at bay. At least, I tried to cling to the path. In the course of defending myself against mosquitoes (read: flailing arms about and slapping myself), I managed to trip and as I went down got tangled up in one of my hiking poles. By the time I hit the ground I was so snarled up I couldn't even figure out how to extricate myself from the mess I'd made of my pack, my poles, and my person.

Amazingly enough, I did not fall off the trail and down the cliff face, but the expectation of doing so had made me cry out loudly in fear and surprise. Now that I was immobilized by my straps and poles, I didn't worry too much because Knut would surely have heard my shout and come running back. But when I twisted my neck around to look forward, all I could see was his usual jaunty step taking him farther down the path.

I carefully reached up and unbuckled my sternum strap, then down to release my hip belt. Now I was able to shake my shoulder loose of its strap enough to dislodge the hiking pole that had somehow inserted itself between my pack and body. Once that was done I looked up again and saw Knut hustling toward me. He helped me the rest of the way to my feet.

I fell more than any other hiker I ever met, but every single time Knut treated it like a serious event worthy of his complete attention. I appreciated that. I expressed my surprise that this time he hadn't come sooner. "Didn't you hear me yell?"

He looked a little sheepish. "I heard something, but I thought it was a marmot squeaking." We both burst out laughing. If I hadn't already been christened NightinGail, I'm sure my trailname would have been given there.

The next day brought us a path rimmed with spiny, snow-capped peaks and alpine passes providing smoke-free views. A bout of diarrhea damaged my ability to enjoy what would have otherwise been one of my top 10 days on the trail. On top of this, a fatigue unlike anything I'd experienced since the High Sierras set in just as raw blisters made a sudden reappearance to boot! Fittingly enough, that night it rained on us, though not until we were safely inside the tent.

Chill now saturated the mornings, but happily the precipitation more or less stopped by the time we broke camp. The cold and the damp must have adversely affected my muscles, for when I swung the pack onto my torso, my back protested in a chorus of spasms. I grimaced with pain, but didn't say anything about it because I figured that, like all the other minor injuries one endures on the trail, this would pass after I walked around long enough for something else to start hurting more. I had only gone a few yards, however, when I realized that things were really out of whack.

We couldn't afford to take a day off because we had to meet Knut's cousin Arlene and her friend Barb the next day at a highway 38 miles distant. I clenched my teeth through no more than a couple miles before asking Knut to help me remove my pack so I could take some ibuprofen and try some stretches. I lay down on the ground and gently did a few exercises I had learned in yoga. I could tell they were helping, but only minimally. I was by now in tears from the pain. I could only make halting movements for fear of setting off a spasm.

One likes to think of oneself as a rugged outdoorsperson. Even in those moments where I had to admit to myself that I could be a bit of a wimp, I still hoped that at least others would think of me as rugged. Knut already knew me too well for that, so I didn't mind crying in front of him, but I was quite embarrassed when Neil (the male half of the Brits) came down the path. He was all kindness, as always, and sat with us while I stretched. He talked about his partner Tanya's own struggles with back pain and the various cures she had found. Prior to starting the hike, her back had seized up so severely she could scarcely walk. Everyone told her not to try the hike, but it proved to be the best thing for her.

At last I decided to give it another try. While I had been talking with Neil, Knut had surreptitiously removed my food bag and loaded it into his own backpack. This was particularly heroic because my food weighed as much as a puppy. I don't remember now what all I had been hauling, but ever since starting out from Snoqualmie I had been promising myself to dump half of it at the first chance.

I found that with enough ibuprofen I could manage all right as long as I didn't make any sudden moves. Limiting oneself to gradual motion is a challenging proposition since the nature of backpacking is that you are treading over uneven ground, sometimes clambering over and around rocks, or hopping across streams. I am prone to tripping over any least trail obstruction, but to do so that day might have had disastrous results for my injured back.

The Brits camped with us that night at the end of a 20-mile day. We found a wonderful spot jutting out into pretty little Deception Lake. A drenching rain soon set in, however, forcing us all in our tents. Knut did virtually everything to set up camp for us, and in the morning he did virtually everything to break it all down again. I deeply hate being useless, but I knew it made no sense to risk further aggravation of my injury by needlessly insisting on doing my bit.

The rain continued relentlessly, except when it would sometimes change to snow—which was much better. I'll walk through snow rather than rain any day. We still had to make 18 miles in order to meet Arlene and Barb. We asked the Brits to look for them and let them know we might be late because of my back.

I hesitate to complain about this day, because in the entire hike it was the one and only time that we trudged through the rain. Most hikers have a lot of rain in the Pacific Northwest, and certainly backpacking in the Midwest, South, or East entails plenty of rain. Having said that, it was an unpleasant day. The temperature stayed low enough that we couldn't stop to rest or we would freeze, so we moved along as quickly as my back would allow.

Arlene and Barb had planned to hike out to meet us. This they did, asking oncoming hikers if they had seen us. To one woman, Barb posed the question, "Have you seen Nightin-Gail?"

"Yes, I've seen them," the woman replied.

"Oh really? Where are they?" Barb enthused.

"I don't mean I saw them today!" the woman answered with surprise. Only later did Barb realize that the woman thought she was being asked about a species of bird. She and Arlene kept going, up the mountain and through the drenching rain. They did encounter our friend Rabbit, but even though she was just a few hours ahead of us, she hadn't seen us at all for days.

When they finally encountered the Brits and got the message that we might be delayed, they turned back and went for lunch. During a lull in the rain as we approached the rendezvous point and obtained a signal, Knut raised Arlene on the cell phone. We learned they had been at a café. I fantasized about the giant sandwiches they were surely bringing us.

Knut, however, had been too polite to beg them for food. When we finally united with them, I had lost virtually all vestiges of a personality to the ravages of hunger, dampness, and pain. I sat numbly in the back of the car like a drowned rat with a lobotomy who can't find the cheese while Arlene drove us a considerable distance to pick up a package I had shipped to a trail angel. From there she took us to Barb's home where our host created a meal so sumptuous that it restored my full personality to all its diminutive glory.

Arlene and Barb are two remarkable women who command respect. Their accomplishments, brilliance, and exceptional good looks would be enough to intimidate lesser beings if not for the fact that these qualities are matched in equal measure by wonderful senses of humor, generosity of spirit, and a genuine interest in other people. They teased us relentlessly for having shown up in such a bedraggled state and with such heavy packs. "We were hiking just fine with nothing but what fit in our pockets. But I guess we are a bit more rugged than you."

The next day, we took a glorious rest day. As always, chores like shopping, laundry, and catching up on email consumed the bulk of the day. But by sunset we were again seated around the table for another unbelievable supper.

Afterward, we had a bit of singing which included some of Arlene's original songs—a real treat! I later had her teach me one of her songs so I could have new material for when I returned to the trail, though I never could make it sound like she did.

Knut made an effort to brag on me by saying that I too had written some nice songs. He encouraged me to sing one. I nervously launched in, but somewhere early in the first verse, the dog joined in. If I stopped, he stopped. When I started again, the dog too began howling in tones only somewhat more melodious than my own, if I do say so myself. It was a neat, if humiliating, parlor trick.

In the morning, Barb once more indebted us to her by producing a hearty pancake breakfast before Arlene returned us to the trail. I would be hard pressed to think of two nicer people.

From the beauty of these trail angels to the beauty of the Washington wilderness, the trail never disappointed. Even with the smoke that often continued to obscure views, the glory of autumn descending on ragged peaks overwhelmed me. The larches turned golden and the huckleberries blanketed the mountainsides in scarlet.

Aside from lingering but diminishing back pain, the only thing marring the delight of being back on the trail was frequent encounters with the Gay Caballeros. These three men were universally loved on the trail for their good taste, rough witticisms, and most of all their harmonious singing. Unfortunately, these world travelers adored Norway and Norwegians. And unlike some they could not be fooled into thinking I was of that race.

Whatever few flaws Knut might have, low self-esteem is not among them. With the adulation now being heaped upon him, his head began to swell to such proportions that I feared for his ability to make it through tight spaces. "Do you think I should change my trailname to God?" he asked me. I glared back.

To add insult to injury, the Gay Caballeros had it in for Wisconsin. If you have ever been on the receiving end of the lacerating wit of certain gay men in a fit of scorn, then you know that self-defense is not an option. All I could do in the face of such ridicule was to tuck my tail between my legs and lick my wounds. Even my friend Train ganged up with them.

"NightinGail is the sweetest girl," he said. "But she just hasn't seen the rest of the world. My family in Missouri is the same way. They think Missouri is great." I figured he was trying to show off to the very attractive Caballeros, so I refrained from putting him in his place. I am, after all, a sweet girl.

Of course, no one can actually be upset at the Gay Caballeros, they are too full of song for that. Plus, one of them had given me a bunch of cookies once.

When we passed the 2,500th mile, we felt unstoppable. Only one more resupply point remained between us and Canada. We worked our way past the magnificent and appropriately named Glacier Peak. That same night two owls swooshed past our campsite at dusk. Then we closed in on the Siuttle River. This entire area had been subjected to severe flooding a few years earlier, and a bridge across the river had been washed away. Hikers had been taking their lives into their own hands by crossing on a precarious log jam. But this year, trail maintainers unveiled a brand new bridge to span the deep, fast-moving waters. Grateful as we were, the old log jam route tempted us to try our hands, as that would save us about five miles.

It's funny how saving five miles can seem like something worth doing when one has already gone 2,500 miles. We asked some southbound section hikers about it, and they told us we would be crazy to do anything but take the safe bet with the new bridge. We came to our senses and kept to the new and official path. En route, we passed a fallen tree whose rings had been counted by someone going before. According to a note on the wood, the tree had endured 658 years. Our lives are but a blip.

We also passed the father/son duo of Chili and Pepper. They had already hiked the Appalachian Trail and now were conquering the PCT. It had been a hard hike for them in many ways, with Chili, the adolescent son, suffering from shin splints and other painful injuries. But he is one of those people who bears all things cheerfully and invariably raises the spirits of everyone around him. The only thing that did not raise our spirits about their presence on this particular evening was that they were camped in the last likely site before the bridge. We ended up pitching our tent in a level spot underneath the new bridge and passed the evening trying to pretend that the white clumps scattered about weren't really toilet paper.

We were happy to be up and out in the morning. When, following the wonderfully built new path, we reached a point where we would could almost see the old log jam, we understood we'd exercised good judgment in taking the bridge. The problem with the log jam was not purely the difficulty posed by crossing the raging river, but that the bank had been so washed away that I'm not quite sure how a hiker would have gotten out of there after making it through the currents. One would have had to either walk downstream for some considerable distance to find a reasonable path or somehow clamber up a vertical wall of scree. I'm sure stronger, more determined people than me could have managed it, but I was happy to stick to the path.

We hovered on the cusp of North Cascades National Park, a location so perfect I could have spent weeks right there. I had been to this area once before and had always told people it was the most beautiful place I had ever been. Since starting this hike, however, I was wondering if seeing it through eyes that were already saturated with a string of beauty reaching all the way back to Mexico would cause me to rethink my opinion. But no. If you can, go to North Cascades Park. (But bring good rain gear! It was here that I had become hypothermic several years earlier.)

We entered the park near a strange little bus stop. The shuttle down this dirt road runs a few times a day to the town of Stehekin, reachable to backpackers by bus and to the rest of the world by a four-hour ferry ride on stunning Lake Chelan. We planned to catch the 12:15 shuttle in for the last resupply of the trip.

As we descended the last couple miles, we heard the sound of running behind us. Turning to see, I found K8, a wonderful hiker from San Diego. She had started the trail with her mother, who was making something like her fourth attempt to complete the trail. Everyone was pulling for her to make it all the way this time, but finally she (the mother) had to leave the trail when her knees wouldn't go anymore. K8 decided to continue on her own to finish. That morning, her pack was light, the trail was gentle, and for some reason she just felt like running instead of hiking. So she was trotting along, but stopped to say hello to us. She was followed closely by Sunny, also running.

I hadn't seen Sunny since about mile 600 when he had made off with Nimblefoot's hiking poles. K8 had never met him before that morning when, not realizing he was deaf, she had asked repeatedly if he would mind stepping aside so she could jog by him. He, however, had no idea she was behind him. Finally she took her hiking pole and gave him a little whack to get his attention to ask him to move. When she got around him, he must have thought that they were running late for the shuttle, because he started running too. As we all stood there together, K8 explained to him that she was just running for fun. Sunny is an excellent lip reader and understood clearly. Nonetheless, when she set off again, Sunny for reasons of his own continued to run too. Now, K8 is a blonde bombshell of a woman and I'm certain she has all kinds of men figuratively running after her, but this may have been the first time one literally ran after her.

We mounted the bus and soon I had my one and only bear sighting of the entire trip, when the driver pointed out the smallish ursine showing us her backside as she rushed for the cover of the forest.

The resourceful community of Stehekin requires its guests to adjust certain expectations. For example, the tiny post office was so overwhelmed by the resupply packages coming in for hikers that I waited in line for well over an hour to speak to the clerk. When my turn finally arrived, the clerk regretted to inform me that he now had to stop taking customers because the ferry would be leaving soon and he needed to be sure the day's outgoing mail was on that boat.

I thought about abandoning the project of retrieving my box, but the food for sale in town was of an extremely limited and expensive nature. While I labored over acquiring the package, Knut struggled to get us checked into a hotel. They seemed to be short-staffed and kept promising our room was about to be ready, but the wait dragged into hours. The day's hot temperature contributed to a mounting sense of annoyance. By the time we finally got these two usually minor logistics worked out, we were downright crabby. Whenever I think about being in a bad mood on the trail, I can't help but feel silly. We were in a remote town on a gorgeous lake surrounded by snow-capped mountains. I'm dumbfounded at my ability to find fault in this situation.

In any case, grouchiness did not remain long. We dined that evening at the Stehekin Valley Ranch. The meal carried a $20 price tag, but since it was of an all-you-can-eat variety, I think it's safe to say we got our money's worth. As I sat there shoveling in the roasted potatoes, cornbread, greens, steak, and lemonade, I suddenly had the sorrowful realization that since this was the last all-you-can-eat meal on the trail, I would probably never again eat this much at one sitting for the rest of my life.

The next morning before taking off, I visited the ranger station to get a permit to camp that night in the boundaries of the National Park. This is virtually the only spot on the entire trail that is not covered by the thru-hiker permit. It's quite a marvel that we had hiked almost the entire 2,667 miles with only one permit—and a free one at that! People hiking less than 500 miles have to pay for permits at every national park and sometimes state parks and other jurisdictions, but those of us hiking long distances just kept moving. It's quite a privilege. However, the North Cascades National Park manages this particular stretch of trail with certain restrictions in force to preserve the ecosystem, namely limiting camping to designated sites. They ask backpackers to pick up a free permit identifying their campsite for the night. The ranger station lay only one block away, and the whole process took no more than a minute. The effort was further rewarded by exposing me to exhibits on the park as well as local artwork hung in a gallery within the station.

Although nothing could have been easier than getting this free permit, the majority of hikers had an astonishingly bad attitude about it. All kinds of false information circulated into rumors that the permit was expensive or difficult to obtain or that they would force you to stay at a campsite you didn't want to stay in. On top of that, many seemed to feel that we thru-hikers were simply above having to obtain permits. I suppose that after five months of being treated as marvels by so many people, both strangers and friends, many of us would indeed inevitably come to feel that we were some sort of special class of people deserving special treatment. Whatever the reason, few among the crowd in which I circulated got the permit, opting instead to hike the entire 20 miles out of the park. Twenty miles, of course, is not a long day, but since the shuttle wouldn't drop us off until noon and since our packs were full and the terrain steep, it was certainly more than most would otherwise have cared to go before darkness fell at its ever earlier hour. A couple hikers decided to set up camp without a permit and were caught by a very nice ranger who explained that they would not be permitted to camp within the park. They told this story a little sheepishly, perhaps feeling a bit bad about making this ranger conduct one of the unpleasant aspects of her job.

From Stehekin, we slowed down and took our time to the border. The weather was good and we had plenty of time before meeting my friends Gabriela and Joaquin, who were picking us up in Canada. So we did 16-mile days and made camp early. The fall colors of the larches and huckleberries began to cloak the mountains in a new kind of beauty, even as the flowers died away. The occasional lingering blooms of the lupines and small-flowered paintbrush cheered me, as these species had been with me the entire stretch of the trail, from the deserts of Southern California to the heights of the Sierras to the meadows and forests of northern Washington. They had become old friends.

With the shorter mileage, I took more time to let Knut get ahead of me and to stop in my tracks to listen to that rarest of sounds—complete silence. In the middle of the day even the birds and the beasts usually kept quiet, so if I didn't move, nothing but an almost dizzying stillness came to my ears.

Taking the last five days of hiking at a leisurely pace was one of the best decisions Knut and I made. Neither of us were eager to end our hike nor to draw our days of companionship to a close. By now, my body—especially my feet—frequently reminded me of the miles I had put on them, and Knut suffered fatigue from the cumulative hiking and poor diet, but still we were not eager to get off the trail. And although I think we both knew we were not likely to be destined for a long-term relationship, we certainly had grown very fond of each other and were not in a rush to part ways. So while others hurried past us to the border, we savored each day with long breaks, early camps, and leisurely walking.

I am usually able to sleep like a rock under any circumstance, but perhaps the notion that this wonderful trip was all about to come to an end wore on my mind in unseen ways. I found myself suddenly unable to sleep well. A happy result of the insomnia was that I witnessed falling stars streaking across the sky night after night.

On September 21, we arrived at Hart's Pass and the last road before Canada. For a legal border crossing via the PCT, a hiker has to request a special permit from Canada. People who choose not to get this permit typically make the crossing, then instead of hiking deeper into British Colombia and returning to the U.S. by car, opt to backtrack to this Hart's Pass. I admit I hoped that someone from civilization might be waiting at Hart's Pass to pick up a friend coming back from the border. Such a person, I speculated, might have a bit of food or a beverage for someone like me.

My hopes were more than fulfilled. A ridiculously good-looking young man had set up camp there with vast quantities of food and beverage all for passing hikers. We stayed the better part of the morning eating bratwurst and drinking pop.

We at last roused ourselves back into our packs and ascended out of the pass. Partway up, I heard the clip-clopping of hooves behind me. Looking back, I saw a bridle-less mule with no rider. I stepped aside to let it pass, and it then stepped around Knutella as it went trotting along northward toward Canada. I sort of worried about it and about its owner, but I had a feeling we hadn't seen the last of it. Sure enough, about an hour later it came trotting back south. That afternoon, I ran into a guide leading some hunters back from an excursion and asked him if he had lost any mules. He said he had about 40 that range freely in that area, so I guess this one just wanted to get away from the pack for a little bit and check out the PCT.

That evening as dusk fell we had the great pleasure of once more seeing our friends Gourmet, Rabbit, and Train, all three on their way back from the border. Train, having fulfilled his odd commitment to wear wedding dresses for the entire hike, now clad himself happily in pants. All three looked joyous to have reached our shared destination. The occasion evoked bittersweet feelings since I knew I might never see these wonderful companions again, but mostly we celebrated the joyousness of realizing how far we had all come together. I was especially thrilled to share this moment with Gutsy Rabbit, since I had been hiking with her off and on ever since mile 140.

While we sat together, somehow Gourmet mentioned the name of another hiker named Clay. "You know Clay? I have his sunglasses!" I exclaimed. I related how I had obtained them at Walker Pass those many months earlier and how my efforts to contact him had not been fruitful. Gourmet said he had his contact info and that if I would give him the sunglasses, he would send them on to Clay. I admit I was sorry to lose the glasses, but relieved to have them off my conscience.

We at last made our final farewells, each of our two parties camping farther up the trail, but heading in opposite directions.

The next morning brought us an exhilarating, odd feeling—this was the day we would cross into Canada. The temperature was cool, and the landscape alight with inexpressibly gorgeous autumn colors. With mysteriously-shaped clouds above, we could not have asked for a more glorious way to finish our hike. In the morning we met K8, joined for the day by her mother and sister, coming back from the border, but otherwise were alone all day.

A 10-foot wide strip of clear-cutting denotes the boundary between the countries. At times, the switchbacks brought us very near this boundary and we could have easily crossed into Canada sooner if we had wanted, but we were in no rush and preferred to enter the country on the trail.

When we at last saw the border crossing, we paused, looked at each other, joined hands and jumped together into the Great North.

A metal obelisk at the crossing contained a chamber in which an earlier hiker had placed a piece of poster board and markers with the request that hikers leave their name and draw a small picture representing something about themselves on the hike. I drew a little bird flying above my trailname: NightinGail.

When I had set out more than five months earlier, I doubted I would ever achieve this moment. Yet I had tried, and here I had prevailed.

We stayed long enough to savor the moment and take photos, then pushed happily on to make camp. No sooner had we crossed into Canada than a grouse strutted along the trail. It was of a species we had not encountered on the previous 2,667 miles—truly we were in a new land. We pitched our tents just north of the border and in the morning hiked the nine miles to Manning Provincial Park, where we got a room at the lodge and awaited the arrival of my dear friends Gabriela and Joaquin.

These dear friends treated us like royalty. They took advantage of the trip to enjoy the nature, and together we spent a day canoeing, hiking, even playing pool. Mostly we laughed, discussed the state of the world, and shared news about friends. With happy hearts, they took us back to the United States, where further adventures awaited my Norwegian friend and me.

Indeed, further adventures await us all.

Epilogue

I had set out on the Pacific Crest Trail in search of solitude and to challenge my skills as a navigator. I also wanted to improve my technical abilities on snow and ice. I achieved none of these things, yet my hike was a complete success. The hike made me feel like a success.

Knut and I spent another month together, taking in additional treasures such as Yellowstone and the Badlands. He returned home to Norway, where I visited a month later. Together we traveled to Turkey to hike a bit with Heesoo, who had moved to Istanbul upon completing his hike. Then, while Heesoo and his wife bicycled in Spain, we stayed in their apartment. There, we definitively broke up on the most amicable of terms. Since then we have hiked together in the Alps and recently completed about 1,500 miles together in Norway.

The Brits recently combined end-to-end hikes of Britain and Ireland. Portrait, Castle, AquaMan, and Train set out on the Continental Divide Trail. Memphis moved to Finland to pursue a career as an international wilderness guide and returned to hike the CDT. Frost and Lone Wolf hiked the CDT that year as well. Gourmet recently completed a thru-hike of the Pacific Northwest Trail to raise funds for cancer research in honor of a hiker named Astro who hiked the PCT after nothing was successful in putting his cancer into remission. Astro died not long after the hike.

At first I felt restless when I heard about all the hikes underway while I sat at home. But as I reconnected with my 40 acres of heaven in northwest Wisconsin, I began to develop a sense of appreciation that I was no longer constantly on the move. I love seeing the seasons unfold day by day. My long distance hiking yen will certainly be indulged again in the future, but I'm enjoying more proximal treasures now, such as the Boundary Waters, Porcupine Mountains, and Chequamegon National Forest. And I'm putting down roots in other ways too, including getting married.

The most enduring change the hike provoked has been a sense of optimism. Something about finally pursuing and achieving a long-held dream has made me happier than I could have imagined. That happiness colors how I see everything. Although I have my struggles and my bouts of sadness, they seem manageable. They don't seem as hard as hiking through the desert.

I hope I can someday do as much for other people as friends and strangers did for me to allow me to achieve this dream. If this book has inspired you in any way, I count that as a small start to make good on a large debt.

CPSIA information can be obtained
at www.ICGtesting.com
Printed in the USA
LVHW02s0132191217
560223LV00042B/2563/P